PARENTING YOUR ADOPTED OLDER CHILD

HOW TO OVERCOME THE UNIQUE CHALLENGES AND RAISE A HAPPY AND HEALTHY CHILD

BRENDA MCCREIGHT, PH.D.

NEW HARBINGER PUBLICATIONS, INC.

Publisher's Note

This publication is designed to provide accurate and authoritative information in regard to the subject matter covered. It is sold with the understanding that the publisher is not engaged in rendering psychological, financial, legal, or other professional services. If expert assistance or counseling is needed, the services of a competent professional should be sought.

Distributed in the U.S.A. by Publishers Group West; in Canada by Raincoast Books; in Great Britain by Airlift Book Company, Ltd.; in South Africa by Real Books, Ltd.; in Australia by Boobook; and in New Zealand by Tandem Press.

Copyright © 2002 by Brenda McCreight
New Harbinger Publications, Inc.
5674 Shattuck Avenue
Oakland, CA 94609

Cover design by Salmon Studios
Cover image by Mel Curtis/Getty Images
Edited by Sheila Freeman
Text design by Michele Waters

ISBN 1-57224-284-1 Paperback

Printed in the United States of America

New Harbinger Publications' Web site address: www.newharbinger.com

04   03   02

10   9   8   7   6   5   4   3   2   1

First printing

Contents

Introduction

Adoption, like most social institutions, has changed with the times. In 1978, our family underwent our first adoption application and home study. Women were wearing shin-length skirts with knee-high boots and men were growing long sideburns and sweating in polyester shirts. Now, as we finish yet another home study to adopt our eleventh and twelfth children, women are more likely to be wearing pants, and men are back to cotton shirts and short hair. The process of adoption, including the profiles of children available and the means of adoption, has changed, too.

Secrecy

The secrecy that surrounded our oldest son's origins is becoming a thing of the past. Open records and the burgeoning search and reunion industry allow adopted children to reconnect with their biological families. One of our older sons recently shared an apartment with his birth siblings while they were all getting established in a nearby city. Our children all know their names as they were on their original birth certificates and each of them has pictures of birth moms and dads; some even have regular contact with birth family.

Who Is Being Adopted?

The decreasing number of healthy Caucasian infants available for adoption has also had a significant impact on the face of adoption. These babies, while still sought by many, have become the least available in North America. Many Caucasian parents adopt children from different racial or ethnic origins, or decide to adopt children older than two years of age.

Today, many adoption agencies are set up solely to find families for the type of children who used to live invisible lives in institutional settings. That is, children who are older than two years; babies and children of color; infants, toddlers, and teens from third world, or eastern European nations; and children who have a suspected or diagnosed disability.

Who Is Adopting?

The personal and economic characteristics of people who adopt are also changing. Our first social worker was very concerned with how much money we made. Our current social worker began the home study with an information session on how much financial assistance is available to us if we choose to adopt a child with "special" needs. Changing social trends and advancing technology have also altered the concept of who may adopt and which children are considered available for adoption. Children of all ages and races from all over the world are now placed with single parents, older parents, gay and lesbian couples and singles, unmarried couples, physically challenged parents, etc. If you, as a prospective adoptive parent, are turned down by your local state or provincial adoption agency, you have the option of applying to a multitude of private agencies that place children from dozens of different countries into adoptive homes.

The Internet

The Internet is a change in technology that has had a major impact on adoption. The World Wide Web has allowed adoption agencies and adoption facilitators to publicly advertise individual children who are available for adoption around the globe. Children and teens whose age, needs, or geographic location once isolated them from potential families are now presented on the Internet so that your heartstrings are tugged toward them. You and I can see the shining eyes of a little girl from a country halfway around the world and make an initial decision about whether or not we might be family for the child before ever talking to a social worker.

The Internet has allowed large and geographically diverse groups of parents to form information and support networks that are gradually taking some of the control of the adoption process out of the hands of professionals and placing it into the hands of adopting parents. This can have the effect of turning us, the adoptive parents, into our own case managers. We can now go online to find out, directly from other parents, the facts about children available in other states, provinces, or countries; which agencies best suit our needs; which social worker to use for the home study; costs; which books to read; the adoption laws of any country; and which therapies to try.

Why I Wrote This Book

Changes in society, such as drug abuse and economic downturns, have increased the number of children waiting to be placed in permanent adoptive families. In response, local and federal governments are making it easier for people to adopt children who are older and they are providing the long-term financial support that is so crucial to supporting high needs children. Globalization makes it possible for couples and singles to adopt orphans from an increasing number of countries. While these factors make more children available to adoptive parents, more parents find themselves raising older children who have mild to severe behavioral problems. Older children often enter into a new family with a host of issues that neither the placing agency nor the adopting family fully understand or anticipate. Many home study models are based on factors that lead to successful parenting in families formed through birth, rather than aspects of family life that are unique to successful families formed through adoption. As the prospective parent, you may believe that an older child will flourish in the solid foundation of your family. But the truth is, for some children, your solid, loving family foundation, with its structure, affection, predictability, child-centered activities, and lack of crises, is so alien that their only hope for psychological survival is to re-create the familiar unpredictability and emotional isolation that have afflicted their lives. The child's attempt to re-create the familiar can wreak havoc on those who are unprepared and untrained to respond to these sometimes alarming behaviors.

I wrote this book because I know how hard it is to raise children who did not begin their life in your home. I know that for most families created through older child adoption, family life is a daily carnival ride that carries the participants through frustration, joy, failure, and success. Most families are able to stay together throughout the ride and find satisfaction in the process.

The parents who succeed are not better parents, nor do they adopt children who are easier to raise. Rather, successful families have adequate information, realistic expectations, and appropriate support. They have learned about the challenges and they have experimented with techniques and supports that have enabled them to find joy and meaning in their adoption-created family.

Who Should Read This Book?

This book may be useful for parents who have adopted a child who is not a newborn, or who have adopted a child from another country. This book will also be helpful to foster parents who are trying to increase the success of behavioral interventions for the children in their care. Therapists may also find that this book enhances their own understanding of the needs and challenges common to families who adopt older children.

How This Book Can Help You

This book can help you to increase your coping skills while facing the challenges of older child adoption. The techniques presented here are nonintrusive and can be undertaken without professional monitoring, although they are particularly useful as a supplement to qualified therapy.

If, like many adoptive parents, you live in an area of the country that does not have a therapist who specializes in adoption, you may want to suggest this book to the therapist your child and family are seeing so everyone involved shares the same approaches and the same understanding of what you and your child are going through.

How to Use This Book

This book can be used as an additional support for families who are in therapy, for families whose therapist doesn't specialize in adoption, or for families who do not have access to any therapy at all. The suggestions provided will generally work for children of most age groups with only minor modifications. As you know, older children do not usually function consistently at their chronological age. One day a child may seem very sophisticated and world weary, and the next day the same child can appear to have returned to early childhood. The techniques presented here are flexible. You'll find approaches that are suitable for young children, for teens, or for teens who need to be treated like younger children. You can tailor the techniques for your child depending on their moods, needs, and behaviors.

You may find it helpful to read the overview provided for each of the challenges before trying the techniques so that you can consider if the label, or diagnosis, for that challenge fits your child.

If you feel uncertain about trying any of the suggestions listed here, it's important that you respect your hesitation and try only those that you feel comfortable with and that you believe will help your unique older child.

CHAPTER 1

Facing the Challenges

Your family is unique. Your older child is special. However, when you get together with other families who have adopted older children, you probably find that you can talk for hours about the similar challenges you are facing. These challenges can be exciting as well as frustrating, but they will not be overwhelming if you are effectively prepared and adequately supported.

The Child's Challenges

Your child may be facing many challenges that get in the way of his ability to meld into your family. Several of these challenges are listed below:

- An underdeveloped ability to attach, or bond, to a new family

- Unresolved grief issues

- Organic learning and behavior disorders caused by the birth parent's use of drugs, alcohol, or tobacco, or prenatal malnutrition

- A history of physical and/or sexual abuse

- Culture shock, culture loss, and overstimulation

- Problems with identity formation in the teen years

- An underlying mental illness

Your Challenges

The obstacles to success in older child adoptions are not all the result of the child's behaviors. You may have issues and beliefs that make it difficult for your family to reform when the new child enters:

- A belief that love is enough to heal the child and maintain the family
- An expectation that you can live and function like a family formed through birth
- A lack of peer support and respite
- Unresolved issues of grief and loss
- Unresolved past trauma similar to that of the child you are adopting
- Unrealistic expectations about your child's abilities
- Unrealistic expectations about how soon after the placement you will feel like a "family"
- Financial restraints that complicate the changing needs of your family
- Your other children who are unprepared to accept the new child

Six Key Strategies for Overcoming Challenges

These challenges can create fears and stumbling blocks that eventually wear down even the most committed parents and children. But the challenges are not insurmountable. Six elements hold the key to a successful older child adoption:

1. Acquiring knowledge about the needs of the child
2. Becoming skilled in meeting those needs
3. Developing patience
4. Emphasizing commitment to your child, not just love
5. Embracing the adoptive relationship as a lifelong bond
6. Facing the facts, and accepting the child for who he is now

Developing the skills to achieve these six key elements can be complex and difficult, but not impossible.

1. *Acquiring Knowledge*

The first strategy, *acquiring knowledge,* is easier today than it was before the development of the Internet. I remember the days when only psychologists and psychiatrists used terms like "attachment disorder" or "sexual intrusiveness." Knowledge of adoption and its challenges was the realm of those few professionals who dedicated their lives to the field and of the few committed adoptive parents who formed associations and printed newsletters. These individuals and groups worked hard to share knowledge through books and conferences, but that knowledge was often unobtainable for those of us who could not attend conferences due to distance or cost, or because they had problems finding a competent sitter.

There were a few books available about adoption, but they were often published by small companies that did not have extensive distribution branches or publicity budgets. The newsletters, often advertised only within the particular state or province, tended to reach mainly those families who were already actively involved in a support network. Luckily, things changed Newsletters and adoption magazines are no longer small, simple information and support pages. Today, they are likely to be sophisticated enterprises. Some aren't linked to an organized adoption group, but stand alone as magazines similar in size and quality to those sold at supermarket checkouts. E-mail newsletters deliver weekly or monthly information on the latest happenings in the adoption community. Articles, books, advice, and support on attachment, fetal alcohol syndrome, oppositional defiant disorder, Down's syndrome, and other conditions are now as close as the family computer. A drawback of e-mail newsletters is that they make both accurate and inaccurate information equally available.

2. *Becoming Skilled*

Becoming skilled is also easier than in the past because of the explosion of information and the increased professional understanding of why some behaviors occur. For example, before we understood the role that attachment plays in a successful adoption, there was little parents could do to create that necessary bond. Now, as the knowledge of this issue grows, techniques to enhance attachment can be more easily learned and applied in most families. Fetal alcohol syndrome was also virtually unknown to most of us just fifteen years ago. Today, the information, while discouraging to some, is easy to access, and more therapists are beginning to teach parenting and behavioral techniques that can improve the long-term outcome for people with this challenging diagnosis.

Parents are also becoming more skilled at deciding when to accept drug treatment for children with attention deficit disorder and bipolar disorder. A decade ago, these disorders left many families bewildered about why their child would act out. Now, greater understanding of how the brain is involved in these conditions allows parents and practitioners to administer medications to reduce symptoms and allow the child to learn how to manage his or her life.

Adoption support groups, created and run by adoptive parents willing to share their skills and knowledge with others, are available throughout North America. Groups often provide general information on the topic of adoption, as well as specific information on topics of interest to families. Often, the larger organizations sponsor many smaller, informal sub-groups so that families can find a supportive ear and a few tips on how to cope with the problem of the day.

3. Developing Patience

Developing patience is easier for some of us than for others. Just as our children all have their own unique personalities, so do we! Some of us are born with patience, others have developed it over the years, and still others find this an evolving goal that is always just one step ahead of us. Yet, patience is crucial to adoption success as an older child triggers and manipulates the emotions of each member of a family. It can take years for an older child to relax enough, trust enough, and heal enough that she can finally feel like she is part of her adoptive family. In the meantime, we parents require enough patience to hang in there through those years and to step back from the dreams we had of how our ideal family would function.

4. Emphasizing Commitment over Love

Emphasizing commitment, rather than love, is a key element to long-term success in an adoptive family. The feeling of love can be elusive to us parents during times of prolonged stress and unrewarding parent/child relationships. Our child, too, may find it easier to love us at some stages rather than others. Still, if commitment is a sacred and articulated value within the family, then your child will learn from you how to hold on as the adoption relationship undergoes the twists and turns of family life.

5. *Embracing Adoption as Lifelong Bond*

Adoption is truly a *lifelong bond.* Children, unlike furniture, clothing, cars, etc., are nonreturnable items. Sometimes the needs of a child are beyond what a family can provide. Regardless of training, support, experience, and love, a child may need an environment other than a family home to heal from past trauma or even to protect the community. However, when that happens, the child doesn't have to be emotionally ejected from your family. Treat a troubled adoptive child as you would a birth child who needed extraordinary help. You can have visits, write letters or e-mail, or talk on the telephone. It does not matter that the connection you maintain is tenuous, it only matters that the child understands that he is not alone in the world and that you still claim him as your own.

6. *Facing the Facts*

The final element, *facing the facts,* may be the most difficult for many of us. This means accepting the child as he is in the moment, not for who we hope he will become. He must be made a part of the family despite the challenges presented by even the most outrageous behaviors. A family cannot be constructed on what may happen tomorrow; it must function in the present. The child must learn that he is important to us even though he may be hurting the dog, burning down the garage, and getting expelled from school. We must first face the fact that this may be who he is, then find a way to raise the child. The potential and the love that most of us see lying beneath the challenging behaviors of the child may take years to come to light; in the meantime, we still have to form a family unit.

Some Things Never Change

While adoption changes, the needs of children and parents remain the same. Your child, regardless of his age at the time of placement, needs a safe, permanent, and loving home. He needs healthy discipline, the opportunity to develop academic and social skills, and to believe that he has an important place in your heart. He needs hope.

You, as the parent, regardless of the issues presented by your child, need to know that you are having some kind of positive impact on his or her life. You need to feel that it is not all work, that some of it is fun and rewarding, and you need to feel that you live in a family, however you define that term. Most of us also need to believe that there will be a positive outcome to all of the sacrifice and hard work we put into our children. We need to hope.

CHAPTER 2

Attachment

Attachment is a word tossed around the adoption subculture like a football in a backyard scrimmage. Yet not everyone shares the same understanding of what this term really means. Some believe that attachment means the love that a parent feels toward a child; others believe attachment is the way a child feels or behaves toward a parent. Still others are confused about whether attachment is a fixed state or an ongoing process. There are parents who believe that they cannot raise a child unless there is a clear attachment, while others believe that any child who does not exhibit attachment behavior is a danger to the family and society. Many parents have been led to believe that if the newly placed child does not indicate a clear attachment within a few months, then he has an attachment disorder. However, attachment is not a fixed condition, nor is the child "disordered" simply because he is in a pre-attachment emotional state. A child who is new to a family requires time and shared experiences before he can begin to develop an attached relationship.

To put it simply, attachment is a two-way relationship that exists between the parent and the child. Successful attachment allows the child to learn how to give and accept love in relationships and to develop a healthy sense of loyalty to loved ones. Early childhood attachment forms the basis for all the child's relationships for the rest of his life. Successful attachment helps him learn to trust his parents and himself. Attachment exists in different forms and develops over time in different ways. How quickly it develops will depend on the emotional temperament and experience of everyone in the family.

The Importance of Attachment

Attachment is important because, while it begins at birth, it impacts a person's entire life. A baby's behaviors serve to get the attention of her mother. From the first rooting for the nipple, to the lifting of the arms to be picked up, the child becomes increasingly sophisticated in gaining mother's attention. This fledgling relationship forms the foundation for the baby's ability to trust others and to trust herself. How she learns to relate to her primary caregiver becomes the basis for how she will relate to the world.

The success of this early relationship is important for you as well, because it makes it possible for you to provide and maintain the energy and constant attention required to care for a child, especially a child who is highly dependent. While most of us think that babies are cute, we also know that they are demanding, exhausting, and potentially unrewarding. The attachment process triggers your need to protect the baby and turns on the overwhelming urge to nurture. In turn, these responses increase your capacity to live with the lack of sleep, the temporary loss or change in your sexual and social lives, and the complete change in lifestyle that comes with the addition to your family of a baby or small child. Not only does the attachment process give you an immediate emotional payoff to all of this change and work, it is a crucial trigger for your child's complex brain development.

Attachment and Your Family

For parents who adopt an older child, especially a child with challenging behaviors, waiting for the attachment process to take place can feel overwhelming. While you wait, you experience little, if any, reward. The child may not have any sense of loyalty toward you, so may steal everything you don't lock up. The child may not accept the love and kindness you offer, and may even punish you by biting, hitting, destroying objects, etc. If the child cannot display the behaviors that trigger your parental responses, you are then as unattached as the child.

Children who have an attachment disorder have a different view of how children and adults relate. It is as if the child comes from some other world, where all the rules are different and he is forced to speak a language he has never heard. The child feels powerless to break the secret code that will show him how to speak your language, but he believes that you, the adult, already have this information and are withholding it. Since he perceives you to be powerful and controlling, he behaves in ways that are powerful and controlling. This often leads to a great deal of frustration and anger for you, as you try to establish an appropriate parent/child relationship with a child who has no understanding of how his more dependent role should be played.

Characteristics of Reactive Attachment Disorder

Reactive attachment disorder (RAD) is the proper psychological term, and is generally diagnosed in situations where the child has experienced caregiving that is poor, chaotic, abusive, and inconsistent, and where the child has had multiple caregivers. It is characterized by the child showing disturbing and inappropriate social behaviors including:

- Destructiveness to self or others (including pets)
- Inability to link cause with effect
- Poor relationships with parents/caregivers and peers
- Superficially charming actions
- Poor or infrequent eye contact
- Attempts to control all situations, sometimes by manipulation, sometimes by aggression
- Demanding or clingy behavior
- Stealing and lying
- Low impulse control
- Little cuddly or affectionate warmth with parents (unless he wants something)
- No remorse or conscience
- Hoarding or gorging on food
- Affection toward strangers

These behaviors usually begin to show up before the child is five years of age and are consistent over a long period of time. Some of these characteristics are also common in other psychiatric conditions; however, the main factor that is considered when diagnosing RAD is that the child has a history of changing caregivers.

Is RAD the Same in All Children?

Children who have experienced neglect, abuse, and changing care-givers may have a limited capacity to easily attach to an adult, but not all will develop full RAD. Children who have lived in orphanages or experienced the horrors of war or extreme poverty may also have attachment challenges with or without developing full RAD. However, children with traumatic histories or those who have experienced insti-tutional living probably will have some degree of attachment challenge no matter how deceptively sweet they look in the pictures provided by the agency. The older the child is at the time of the adoption place-ment, the more likely it is that she will face serious obstacles to attach-ing to the adoptive parents.

This means that not only will she have trouble attaching to you, but she won't trigger the protective, nurturing feelings in you that you need in order to continue caring for her if she presents severe behav-ioral challenges. Indeed, such children seem quite skilled at sabotaging your early attempts to bond. They do not do this out of spite or mental illness or even from full RAD. They are terrified or threatened by the unfamiliar feelings created when you attempt to form a close emotional relationship. The child may have lived a life characterized by loss and betrayal, so like any smart person, she protects herself by making sure no one gets close enough to hurt her again. Other children may not be this sophisticated in their emotional processes. It may simply be that the child has been emotionally alone for so long, that he cannot recog-nize a good thing when he sees it. It is as if he does not know how to grab onto, or recognize, the emotional lifeline that you are offering.

We all have different reasons for deciding to adopt an older child. And when the decision is to welcome a child with attachment chal-lenges, most parents are prepared to wait and learn how to help the child achieve attachment. Yet, even the most selfless adopting parent generally wants to create an environment that feels like a family. That is, a parent wants some sense that she is the mom or dad to a child. It is very difficult to stay motivated in the face of behavioral challenges when the child cannot display even the smallest amount of loyalty to, or interest in, the adoptive family.

While not all older children have attachment problems, it is important to understand that an older child will need time to develop a fully attached relationship. Expecting to feel the same about an older child newly placed in your home as you would a baby or children already in your home may create problems. Few parents feel the same joy in the first days of parenting an older child that they may have experienced parenting an infant. You must first get to know the child and she must be given time to experience the loss and grief she may have from leaving her previous caregivers. Children from other cultures, or those who have lived a life very different from the life you offer, may have a difficult time with culture shock. They won't be able to begin the attachment process until they have begun to understand the language and customs of their new home.

Jacinthe's story, below, illustrates how difficult it can be for a child to adjust, even when the new environment is safe and healthy.

Life Lesson: Disrupted Attachment

Jacinthe, age six years, was one of three biological siblings placed together. She and her two younger brothers had been in and out of their mom's care for the first four years of Jacinthe's life. For the past two years they had been in permanent foster care. Jacinthe had been in only one foster home during that time, but it was a busy house in a poor community that had few resources. The foster mother, a very loving and giving elderly woman, always had several children in her home and there was not much time or energy for any one child. Jacinthe's little brothers were only ten months apart in age and clung to each other. They were also cute and cuddly and had managed to find their way into the foster mother's bed most nights. The foster mother, generally too tired to take them back to their own beds, hugged them close. These nighttime cuddles, as well as the boys' relationship with each other, had nurtured their ability to attach. But Jacinthe had always been alone. Forced to act as a single mom when they had lived with their crack-addicted mother, Jacinthe had fed the boys as best she could, changed their diapers when she could find any, and tried to rock them when they cried. When they went into foster care, she gave up her parental duties, and disappeared into the busy household. She behaved well enough in the home to be considered a "good girl," and did well enough in school that her teacher labeled her a good student. No one paid her any particular attention, and she liked that well enough. It was what she had always known.

The adoption was a surprise to Jacinthe. The social workers talked to her about it a lot, but she had not really understood what it meant. When the nice couple came to visit and took her and her brothers out to eat, she was well behaved so she could get more treats. She smiled and said "thank you" as her foster mother had taught.

When Jacinthe and her brothers were in their new home, their parents said she could phone her foster mother whenever she wanted. Jacinthe didn't understand why she would want to do that. Her brothers wanted to call their foster mother almost every night, and they would talk and cry on the phone. Jacinthe talked too, but only because she liked to use the phone.

One day after the children had been in the family a while, the new mother called Jacinthe to come downstairs and watch the dad while he opened his birthday presents. Jacinthe could hear the boys whooping and laughing. She hated it when they got all excited. They always jumped on her and their feet hurt when they landed on her legs.

"I don't want to," she called down from the TV room. "I want to watch my show."

The mother came up the stairs. She had a funny look on her face. She said, "Jacinthe, this is a family birthday. You'll get presents and a cake when it's your birthday and we'll all celebrate with you. The same with your brothers. This time it's Daddy's turn to get the presents and to get a little spoiled."

"No thanks," said Jacinthe as she turned back to the TV.

After a while, the show ended and Jacinthe felt hungry. She could hear the grownups talking and the boys giggling. She remembered the mother had said something about cake so she decided to go down and have some.

The mother was in the kitchen cleaning up the mess from the party. The cake was on the counter.

"I'm hungry now. I'll have some cake," Jacinthe said as she walked over to the table and sat down.

The mother had that weird look again. "No, you won't. You didn't want to be included in the party, so you don't get any of the cake. If you're hungry, I'll fix you a sandwich."

The youngest brother walked into the kitchen. He had chocolate all over his face and hands. Chocolate was Jacinthe's favorite.

"That's not fair. They got some. I want some cake too." She started to cry. The mother wouldn't look at her. Instead she started to wet a cloth so that she could wash the little boy's face. "I want some cake too," Jacinthe said again, her voice louder this time.

"I told you, if you're hungry, I'll make you a sandwich," the mother said.

Jacinthe looked at her brother. He was licking the icing that was stuck to his fingers. She could feel her stomach growling. "I hate you," she yelled, and pushed her brother against the counter. His head hit the door handle and he started to cry. The mother picked him up and turned to Jacinthe.

"Go to your room. You can stay there until supper." Jacinthe did not budge. She wanted the cake. "Move," the mother said. Jacinthe reached around her and grabbed the cake. It splattered on the floor. "Get out," the mother said, barely whispering. Jacinthe left the kitchen and went to her room. She had years of experience being hungry. This was nothing new.

The next day the new mother tried to get close to Jacinthe again. She wanted to fix Jacinthe's hair and kept trying to hug her. Jacinthe hated that. She didn't like the feeling of having someone else's hands on her head, and she hated being held so close that she could feel the other person's skin and breath on her cheek. Most of all, she hated being kissed. She remembered how some of the men her mother brought home had kissed her before they hurt her. She wasn't about to put up with that now that she was bigger.

"Stop pulling, Jacinthe. I don't want to hurt your head," the mother said as she took another piece of the hair and started to comb. Jacinthe tried to pull away again, but the mother had hold of her head and wouldn't let her move. Jacinthe remembered being bitten once by a dog trying to escape her unwelcome grasp. She had let it go quickly. So, she turned around and bit the mother.

"Ouch," the mother yelled. "I can't believe it! You bit me!" The mother threw down the brush and stood up. "Okay, you do your own hair from now on, but don't blame me if the kids tease you about having messy hair."

The adoptive father was also a problem. He kept picking her up and telling her she was his princess. She didn't like that. He was big and when he picked her up it scared her to be off the ground. Finally, she kicked him in the stomach. "Oof," he said, and put her down quickly.

"What's the matter?" the mother asked as she came into the room to find her husband doubled over holding his stomach.

"She kicked me," he said. "For no reason."

"It was the same when she bit me. I think we need to get some help. What if she's really violent, Graham? Do you think she hurts the boys?"

"I don't know," he replied. "But we do need some help. She doesn't seem to care about us or anything. It's like she has no feelings. Maybe she's attachment disordered."

"Well, social services will help us with a therapist. We need to find one right away."

"What do we do in the meantime?" he asked.

"I guess we just keep on doing what we're doing and not crowd her or try to get too close. At least that's what it said in the books I've been reading."

"I didn't think it would bother me this much if they didn't seem to love us. I thought I'd be able to handle it better. The boys are great. They're more than great. But she's just like an empty, angry shell. I don't even feel like talking to her anymore."

"I know. I feel the same way. I just adore the boys, I couldn't bear to let them go."

"Do you think they'd let us adopt just the boys?" he asked. "I know that sounds cruel, but how do we live with someone who is violent? How do we raise someone who doesn't care?"

Overcoming the Attachment Challenge

These are some techniques that adoptive parents can use to counter attachment problems.

Reduce your expectations. Developing an attached relationship may take a long time. In some instances, it may take until the child has reached adulthood. She may need that distance from her early trauma in order to look back and realistically evaluate what you have been offering her all these years. If you feel that you can't possibly wait that long for a child to bond, then you may want to consider a child with an extremely low risk of attachment problems rather than a child who has any of the risk factors. Some parents begin to feel frustrated within a few weeks of living with an unattached child. This can lead to their exerting pressures either subtle or overt on the child. In turn, this can lead to the child pulling further away.

Get a professional evaluation of the degree of attachment problem. Attachment problems can be thought of as existing on a continuum. Children may have some degree of the problem without having full RAD. It is important to understand where your child is on this continuum so that the intervention is appropriate to the need. Be sure your child's therapist evaluates whether you're facing an attachment problem or an adjustment problem that does not involve a psychological disorder.

Play "feet." Feet involves everyone living in the home taking turns having his or her feet and hands massaged by the others. For example, one child or adult lays on the floor, bed, mat, or any place that feels safe. The others each take an extremity and start massaging. Let each child and adult pick their own lotion or oil. While the massage is going on, the people doing the massage focus completely on the massagee and talk about all of his positive attributes, e.g., "I love your hair, Michael. It's so thick and shiny"; or "Joan, you were really nice to the dog today"; or "It made me feel really good to see how happy you were at the birthday party today, Max." Each massage should last, at most, about five minutes. The comfort level of the child or adult receiving the massage should dictate the timing. This technique also allows the family members who are giving the massage to switch over and receive the massage, experiencing unconditional giving.

Sing to your child. At bedtime, sing a song with, or to, your child. Make sure it's just the two of you. Don't share your song with anyone else. A stanza or two is enough. Make it a simple song such as "You Are My Sunshine" or a song from your child's country or culture of origin. This takes the place of the early nursery songs that were not likely sung to her when she was an infant. Sing every night whether or not the child is in trouble for negative behaviors. If possible, try to hold the child's hand, or have her sit on your lap while singing.

Do not isolate your child at time-outs. Have time-out happen at the kitchen table or some other central area in the home so your child or teen stays in contact with you. This prevents secondary problems such as sneaking out of the room or breaking the bedroom window. It also makes it clear to your child that you are not rejecting him. Have a box of Legos or coloring or painting materials handy to occupy the child. Older children can work on a model car, or Barbie hair salon, or homework, while sitting at the table. Sometimes, your child will have to be restrained by you first, before he can sit still. When this happens, hold the child on your lap wherever it is safest to do so, then move him to the kitchen table when he has calmed. Or, the child may be able to sit right away, but may throw or break anything that is put in front of him. If this seems likely to occur, don't give the child anything to do until he has calmed. In fact, having something to do can be the reward for calming.

Most negative behaviors are best handled with only a few minutes of time-out. However, some children get into an emotional state in which they cannot manage their behavior around other people for several minutes, or longer, after an outburst. It is then necessary to lengthen the time-out period until the child regains self-control in order to protect family members and to avoid a repetition of the same negative behavior. It's important that the parent stays in the room with the child during the time-out. Most parents can find something to occupy them: Do the dishes, clean the refrigerator, wash the floor, rearrange the spice cupboard. Do something that is independent of your child but keeps you in proximity.

Use rewards more frequently than consequences. Each time your child gets mad but does not hit or bite anyone or anything, reward her with a point. At five points, she should get a reward such as a small toy. At twenty-five points, she should get a large reward. Don't take points away when the child misbehaves. This reward system may appear to be focusing on material goods, but it is often the only thing the unattached child can recognize as representing affection. Use it as a way to begin showing her your love.

Do not use time with you as a reward. You owe your child the time just because he is a child. He should be learning that he is important and worthy of your attention without having to earn it.

Choose one or two battlegrounds at a time. Trying to change too much too fast is too difficult. If your child is stealing, setting fires, killing small animals, and hoarding food, then focus on the issues that relate to safety and leave the rest for next year. Don't fight your first battles over culture or past ways of living. Fight your battles over issues that really impact your ability to raise your child. Manners and customs are not important in the first few years, but safety and affection are crucial.

Let your child spend time in your bed. The age, stage, and experiences of the child will affect when and how you let your child into your bed.

However, at some point it can be helpful to re-create the early nesting that goes on with parents and infants. This can be done casually by adding a television to your bedroom so that once or twice a week, you and your child watch a show together. Or, you can read to your child in your bed. Everyone should be fully dressed in day clothes, and sitting on top of the bedspread. Some children may need to have their shoes on in order to feel safe enough to want to participate. Children who have been sexually abused may feel this sort of activity is coercive or seductive, so spreading a blanket on the living room floor may suffice until the child feels secure.

A child who is sexually intrusive should not be in your bed for any reason. You may want to let him sit on the bed to watch TV with everyone, but only if you are present the entire time.

Swaddle your child. Wrap your child, or teen, in a large blanket and swaddle him while you hold him on your lap and sing softly. This can be done as a playful gesture or in any noncoercive way that works to get the child involved. You may initially model with another child. Teens respond to this as well as young children. It is often an important part of the infant/parent relationship that the unattached child missed and still needs to experience. Swaddling also gives you the opportunity to share this closeness with the child and to experience the joy of holding an otherwise unholdable child or teen.

Find out what physical contact your child can manage. It is important that your child begin to accept touch from you. If he cannot manage a hug, find out if he can manage having one of his fingers held. If he can manage holding hands, teach him hand hugs (a light squeeze of the hand). Perhaps he can manage to let you rub his back lightly while he is standing up in a neutral room like the den or outside in the backyard. Do not give up. Most children and teens have one or more ways in which they can accept affectionate touch.

Another way to begin touch is to offer to towel dry or blow-dry your child's hair after a shampoo or after swimming. Or, offer to do the shampoo at the sink so that you can touch her head while rubbing in the shampoo. You may have to play detective and find a way of simple touch that is acceptable to the child.

Sit with your child until she falls asleep. This is time consuming each evening, and may need to go on for a year or more after placement, but night time is often a source of significant terror for children with traumatic backgrounds or who have lived in orphanages. This is a concrete way to spend time alone with your child as well as to demonstrate your commitment. Teens can benefit from this, although they may only wish to have the parent present for a short length of time. This should be a silent time, with little or no conversation. You can take a book or knitting or whatever will help to pass the time until the child is asleep. A comfortable rocking chair or a beanbag chair can also help make sitting more pleasant for you. Some children will do better if you can stroke their head or hold their hand. Sitting with your child should happen every night regardless of whether the child has been in trouble.

Find ways to be with your child that do not appear to be play. Some children arrive in an adoptive home with little or no experience of play and are threatened by the closeness that playing with you represents. They may also be overwhelmed with all of the new rules in the house and learning more for play such as board games or hoop games can be too much. Substitute shared activity for play. Try cooking with your child. Even a young child can make milk puddings. Or, try working outside in the garden together. Planting and digging do not have to be done correctly; they have to provide a way for you two to be together. For some, window-shopping may work, or walking the family dog, or any activity in which the talk does not have to be focused on the child and you.

Find ways to play together. If your child can play with you, be sure that there is ample time for this. Children from extremely deprived backgrounds, such as orphanages, may not know how to play. This may be a learning experience as well as a time for bonding. It is likely that your child will need to have toys and recreational activities that are designed for a much younger age.

Feed your child. Find a reason to feed your child either part or all of his meals. Or, when being playful, feed him raisins or orange slices. This should be done in the same playful and considerate manner as is done with an infant of six to twelve months of age. However, the child can be any age, even a teen. It can also be helpful to feed the child or teen with a baby bottle. This can be done while swaddling, or while nesting in your bed.

Help your child cope with peer rejection and social isolation. Children who cannot form relationships with adults generally cannot form friendships with peers. You can help your child by ensuring she has access to socially appropriate clothing (which she may choose not to wear) and has her hair cut and styled in a manner that is socially acceptable to her classmates. If your child has trouble with her peers and no one is going to come to her birthday party, don't invite anyone. Instead, plan something fun and exciting that includes the whole family or make it a special hockey game out of town with Dad. Check at school to see if the child is being teased or tormented by classmates. If she is, work with the school counselor, the teacher and the tormentor's parents to decrease the problem. Help your child learn what to say when she is teased or tell her who she can go to for help if she is being bullied on the playground. If she is the bully, include the school counselor and principal in finding ways to curb her behavior.

Reduce outside contact. If your child is from another culture, has spent time in a residential treatment center or orphanage, or has been moved through a series of foster homes, consider home schooling for the first few months. This will reduce the amount of new data the child has to integrate and create more physical and emotional energy for bonding. Your child can start slowly to socialize by joining Cub Scouts or Brownies, or by taking classes at the local recreation center.

Do not trust your child. Children from traumatic or severely neglectful backgrounds do not have an understanding of "trust," at least not in the way that you understand the concept. Telling a child that it is important that you can "trust" him is a set up for disappointment. Your child has probably never lived a life where he can trust adults or where people trusted him. Consider this word to represent a totally alien concept and then give him a few years in the home before allowing situations where trust may be an issue.

CHAPTER 3

Loss and Grief

Loss is considered to be one of the core issues of adoption culture and it is a profound part of the adoption experience. For many years, this aspect of adoptive culture was unrecognized. It was believed that children forgot their early experiences and did not have any feelings regarding their birth families. And it was believed that most adoptive parents resolved any feelings of loss that they may have experienced about infertility simply by adopting a baby. These myths have been dispelled over the last twenty years by the many adoptive parents, adoptees, and birth families who wanted their grief recognized and respected.

What Have You Lost?

Adoptive parents of older children experience loss if they are choosing to adopt because of fertility problems, or if they cannot wait or afford to adopt an infant. If fertility and infant adoption are not issues and adoption of an older child is a first choice, then there is still the loss of your normalcy that goes with raising children whose life experiences began before the placement. Often, the adoptive parents do not realize this substantial loss until years after the child has joined the family. By that time they find it difficult to identify the feelings and create support.

What Have Your Adoptive Children Lost?

The children, of course, have likely experienced loss in every setting in which they have lived. This includes the loss of their birth parents, siblings, and extended family, the loss of friends, pets, toys, and caregivers. The child may also experience loss when she leaves a negative situation, because even the bad experiences were, at least, familiar.

Children who are older when they are placed for adoption have experienced broader losses. Some children may have experienced the loss of their native language and country or culture of origin. Culture is often more subtle than it appears. For example, an American child who has grown up in a foster home in a large city will face cultural loss if he is placed with a family in a rural farming community. The language is English, but the accents and the use of language will differ. There also are significant differences between urban and rural lifestyles. This type of placement can lead to as severe a sense of loss as a child from a Cambodian orphanage may face when placed with an affluent North American family.

For many children who have moved between relatives or foster homes, the losses have accumulated without ever being identified, acknowledged, or resolved. This can leave the child unable to identify the experience and feelings of loss, because loss is the norm in his life, rather than the exception. He may say that he does not miss anyone or anything from his past, because he has lived so long with hurt feelings that he no longer understands that they are a source of emotional pain and stress. Or, in order to survive, he may have stopped allowing himself to feel the loss. Unfortunately, when people shut off one set of feelings, they shut down many others, too, so your child may be equally shut off from feelings of joy. Sometimes children cope with past losses by refusing to attach to, or care about, anything new that is brought into their lives. This can mean that the child will not allow himself to get close to you or to anything you are offering.

While some children will have lost their ability to feel their own emotions, others may have lost a sense of their right to exist in this world. And for some children, there is also the loss of hope that they will ever get to live in a "normal" family. That is, a family where the children look like the parents and they have always lived together. The child may understand that he could not remain where he was being neglected or abused, and he may be very happy with the family who has adopted him. Still, like you, the neighbors, the schoolteachers, and everyone else, the child knows that a family created through older-child adoption is different from other families.

Recovering From Loss

Loss that is followed by adequate grieving can be resolved at least well enough that you and your child can begin establishing new bonds. However, loss that is denied and grieving that is unsupported can lead to emotional obstacles that prevent the development of new and healthy emotional ties. Unresolved and unacknowledged losses can leave both you and the child fearful of beginning new relationships, because of a belief that the past relationships are still viable or can be reestablished. Loss that is acknowledged and grief that is given support make it possible for the formation of healthy adoptive families.

Stages of Loss and Grief

There are many different theories about the stages of grief but the foundation of most is the work of Dr. Elisabeth Kubler-Ross (Kubler-Ross 1969). She worked with patients with terminal illness and developed her theories by examining how the patients and their loved ones came to terms with impending death. Dr. Kubler-Ross noted that there were definite stages to the grieving process:

- **Denial.** The person refuses to accept that the loss has occurred. Example: "This cannot be true and cannot be happening to me."

- **Anger.** Intense feelings that the condition is not fair and should not have happened. Example: "How could you have let this happen to me? I hate you for that."

- **Bargaining.** Trying to find a way to fix the problem so that the loved one can be restored. Example: "If I can have the loved one back, I will never be bad again."

- **Acceptance.** Example: "I know I can't change it and I will go on."

Others theorists have suggested that there are more stages, including:

- **Shock.** This comes before denial and puts the person into a state of emotional numbness: "I can't think straight and I don't understand what is happening".

- **Fear.** The person is afraid that he cannot live without the loved one and he is afraid of the loneliness that accompanies the loss, "I am afraid I will die if I never see my mom again."

- **Guilt.** This can result from the person feeling that she should have been the one who died, or that if she had been a better baby, her mom could have been a better parent.

These stages do not happen in strict order, and the person can go through each of them many times before getting to resolution.

Over the years, this basic concept of loss has broadened from simply looking at loss that comes from death, to understanding that feelings of loss can come from any major or negative change, particularly when most or all of the change has been out of the control of the person who experiences it.

Symptoms of Grief

Grief is a normal response to loss. Everyone has a different way of expressing grief, but there are some common grieving experiences:

- Difficulty concentrating

- Apathy

- Anger

- Guilt

- Sleep disturbances

- Eating disturbances

- Irritability

- Social withdrawal

- Intense sadness

- Depression

- Numbness

- Feeling lonely, separate from others

- Inability to find meaning or purpose in life

- Mood swings
- Self-injurious behavior
- Memory loss
- Assuming mannerisms or habits of the lost person
- Constantly talking about the lost person

The Impact of Loss and Grief

You may find that a child who was fun and emotionally warm on pre-placement visits suddenly appears sullen and controlling after the first few days of the placement. You may feel you are now seeing the child's true nature and that you have adopted a child who has more problems than you were led to believe. The reality is that often, when an older child is placed in a new adoptive home, the grief brought about by this change overtakes the child's initial excitement. The grief may be a response to the changes, or it may be that the child is missing the foster parents, or it may be that the adoption has forced the child to realize that she will never again live with her birth family. Whatever the reason, the child's experience of grief is greatly at odds with your joy.

Some children may be in a home for quite a while before they begin to act out their grief. Sometimes after months or even years in a new family, a child begins to undergo emotional changes brought about by love and security. When she drops the defenses, or walls, that kept her feelings at bay, she may be overwhelmed with the pain of grief. Because this can happen so long after a child comes to live in the home, it is often unrecognized and misdiagnosed. She does not understand why she has started to feel so bad, and you cannot understand what is causing the sudden anger and acting out. Without appropriate treatment, she can develop depression or may begin to use drugs and alcohol in an attempt to return to the more familiar condition of emotional numbness.

When Emotions Collide

It can be very difficult for you to accept that the event for which you have waited so long is, for your child, a time of heartbreak and stress. When the emotions of the parents and the child are in conflict, the child is at risk for having her experience of grief misinterpreted as an adjustment disorder or an attachment challenge. In order to reduce this risk, the parents must first acknowledge that the child has the right to grieve. The task of adoptive parents is to help the child identify her losses and claim her grief. This takes time and support.

The grieving process may take years to resolve. That does not mean that the child cannot establish meaningful relationships or enjoy her life in the meantime. She can, but only if she is also receiving respect and support for her losses. Sometimes it's difficult to recognize the effects of grief, as Mike and Elaine discover in the vignette below.

Life Lesson: Recognizing a Child's Grief

Mike and Elaine adopted Tyrell when he was five years old. They knew quite a lot about his background, including the fact that he had lived in four different foster homes by the time he was four years old. He had never really known his biological mother or father, but his maternal grandmother phoned him every week and visited him every month, no matter where he lived. Tyrell knew that she loved him, and he loved her, but she was very old and was sick a lot, so she could not take care of him. Still, she gave him someone to cling to and to claim as his own, so Tyrell did not develop an attachment disorder. In fact, he still saw her regularly, after he was adopted by his new parents, Jim and Elaine, who let him call her as much as he wanted and visit on occasion.

About a year after Tyrell moved in, Elaine was putting him to bed one night when she suddenly started to cry. She did not want the child to see her like this, so she hurried through the bedtime story and left the room as quickly as she could.

"Mike," she said to her husband, "we need to talk."

"What is it?" he asked as he turned on the dishwasher. Mike gave the sink a last wipe and sat down at the table. He knew that when Elaine began a sentence with "We need to talk," it was going to be serious. He looked at his watch. Likely he would still be seated here long after the opening kick of the evening football game.

Elaine sat at the table across from Mike. She let the tears flow down her cheeks as she tried to find the words to describe her feelings. "I don't really know what is wrong, but I think I'm failing as a mother to Tyrell. There's something wrong with him."

"Why would you say that? You're a wonderful mother!" Mike exclaimed. "Look at how Tyrell has blossomed this past year. He's grown, he's gained weight, he has friends, he's doing well in kindergarten. What could you have done wrong?"

"I know he's doing well everywhere. But I also know that there is something wrong. It's like there's something missing in him. Some part that I can never reach."

"I don't get it, Elaine. He couldn't be attachment disordered. We've read all about that and he doesn't do any of that acting-out stuff. And he's always been attached to the grandmother. He cuddles us and he has relationships with lots of people. What do you think is missing?"

"That's just it. He's too well behaved. He's like a little robot. I was having tea with my sister today and she spent the whole two hours talking about all the trouble her boys get into all day. And there's nothing wrong with them. They're normal little boys. Tyrell never gets into trouble. He never does anything wrong. And at night, when I tuck him in, it's like a part of him just isn't there. Sometimes I wonder if he's depressed, or scared that we'll reject him."

"I don't think so, Elaine. He's just a good boy. You belong to too many adoption lists. All those other people have really crazy kids; and we get a good one, so you think there has to be something wrong."

"Don't tease me, Mike. There's something wrong with a child who is never really naughty. If he isn't ever really mad, then how can he ever be really happy? Maybe he isn't ever bad because he isn't ever really anything? Have you thought about that?"

Mike was slow to answer. He had not thought about it at all. They had gone through so many years of fertility treatments, then years trying to decide where and how to adopt a child. He had been unsure about adopting an older child because he had read about how so many of them have serious problems. But Elaine had persevered, and when the social worker finally approached them about Tyrell, Mike knew he had struck gold. This little boy had never been exposed to any drugs or alcohol before birth, and was not known to have been abused. He was only in foster care because his parents were killed in a car accident when he was a baby and the only living relative, the grandmother, was too poor and too sick to raise him herself. He had been in a few foster homes, that was true, but that was only because of things going on in the foster homes, like people quitting, or moving. It had taken the social workers a long time to go through the paper work that would make him available for adoption. So, Mike had breathed a sigh of relief and agreed to adopt the child. This last year had been a dream come true. The boy was everything he hoped for. He was sweet and he was well behaved. He liked sports. He was doing well in kindergarten. He was perfect. As that last thought hit him, Mike realized that Elaine was right. The child was perfect. And that was something that no child should ever be.

"I think you may be right, Elaine," he said slowly. "But what could be wrong? Do you think he's depressed? Could he be lonely? Does he need a brother or sister? What are we doing wrong?"

Mike and Elaine took Tyrell to a therapist the next week. Within ten minutes of the first interview, the therapist asked Elaine how Tyrell had dealt with the grief of losing his parents, as well as the loss he had incurred when he moved among foster homes.

"His what?" Elaine asked.

"His grief," the therapist repeated.

"Uh-oh ..." Elaine answered.

Overcoming the Challenges of Loss and Grief

Dealing with loss and grief are important steps to healing and to developing a family identity. Following are some techniques to make this challenge more manageable.

You must consider your own loss. Therapy and support groups can be useful for this and should be undertaken before the child is placed. However, it is never too late to get help with this issue. If you have had other substantial losses in your own life and have never come to terms with them, then this, too, must be considered before there can be success in helping the child move past his loss.

Accept that your joy may conflict with the grief of your child. You should be forthcoming in showing your delight at having your older child join the family. However, you should also understand and acknowledge that your child may not be able to relate to the joy until her grief has been identified and validated, when she is on the way to resolution. This takes time and patience on your part as you must set aside your own need for immediate reward in the parent/child relationship.

Acknowledge the loss with your child. Talk with your child about all the things she has lost in her life, and do this on more than one occasion. These should not be forced conversations, although you will likely have to be the initiator. The correct moments will present themselves, and it's important not to be afraid to enter into, and initiate, these discussions.

Don't reject or fear your child's pain. Most loving parents tend to avoid issues that appear to hurt a child. You may view this as a form of protection. However, in relation to loss, it is important that you make it clear to the child that you can hear how much your child misses the orphanage, or the last foster parents, or the last school, or the previous language, or the birth mother who beat her. Your child's grief over the past can sometimes feel like rejection to you. But you must be able to put your feelings aside. What counts is that your child learns that she can tell you about what she misses and how much it hurts. Sharing feelings of grief can facilitate bonding, and, if she cannot say it with words, she will express it with behavior.

Comfort your child. Let him know that it's all right to sit on your lap and cry when he misses his birth mom, or when he is feeling sad that he can never live at "home" again, or when he is missing a sibling or foster parent. It can be hard for you to listen to a child cry about missing an abusive or neglectful birth parent, but you must take your feelings elsewhere.

Get pictures and photographs. Try to get as many photographs of people from your child's past as possible. Keep them separate from other family pictures for the first year or so, or until your child indicates that she is ready for her life to merge with that of your family. If there are no photographs available, try to get postcards or other types of pictures of your child's city and country of origin.

Use a life book to identify loss. Life books provide a chronicle of your child's life and living situations. They also give a clear picture of what she has left behind. When going through the life book with your child, ask her whom she misses. Ask her if she feels sad when she thinks of the people or places in the book. When she identifies a person as someone she misses, use the opportunity to validate your child's feelings.

Reassure your child that he did not cause his loss. Many children who are in foster care have a belief that they are at fault for the bad things that have happened in their lives. Your child may believe that if he had been a better baby, then his parents would not have taken drugs. Or, he may believe that if he had been a better little boy, then the foster parents would not have gotten divorced and he would not have had to move again. The child may have come to this belief on his own, or he may have been told this in the past. Either way, your task is to constantly reassure the child that he did not have the power or the ability to control what has happened and that it is not his fault that he has lost so many people from his life.

Have your child join a peer group for dealing with loss. It would be best for your child to go into an adoptive children's group, but if there are none in your area, then any counseling group that focuses on loss would be useful. Children are able to normalize each other's experiences better than adults. Your child may need to participate in this type of group at each stage of development.

Have a family candlelighting ceremony. This may be done for your child alone or for each family member. Get several candles and place them in a bowl of sand or rocks or something else that won't catch fire and that will hold the candles upright. As each candle is lit, state who or what it represents. For example, one candle may represent the birth parents, former foster parent, or a beloved pet or toy that had to be left in a former living situation. Don't shy away from major losses your child has experienced in life, such as the death of a parent or family member. However, this ceremony, when done with your child, is not the time for you to mourn the loss of fertility or the loss of not adopting an infant.

After the candles are lit, and child and family members have acknowledged each loss and perhaps said "good-bye" to each part of the past, the candles can be blown out, either one by one or all at once. Something special should then be done with the candles. They can be buried, tossed into the ocean or river, or wrapped up and put in a safe place. Just make sure they are not used again.

A second candlelighting ceremony is part of a ritual that is also useful for building identity. This involves the same procedure with candles, but in this ritual, your child lights a candle for each of the people or things which she feels she has gained. This should not be done to supplant the previous ceremony, but can be added to it to help your child understand the gains that have arisen from the loss.

Write a letter. Your child may wish to write a letter saying "good-bye" to people from the past. This letter may be mailed, hand delivered, put in a bottle and thrown out to sea, burned, buried, etc. Some of the people to whom the child wishes to write may be deceased or their whereabouts unknown, while others can be easily located. The delivery of the letter is less important than the writing of the letter.

Do not add to the loss. Many older children have existing relationships with relatives and foster parents at the time of placement. Some of these people may be very different from the adoptive family and can disrupt the child's ability to settle. Rather than cut them out of the child's life when there are difficulties, mediate and resolve the conflicts or, if all else fails, learn to live with the difficult relationships. Creating fresh wounds by cutting out a demanding grandmother is more likely to send the child back to Grandma than it is to help the child to bond with you.

Consider facilitating contact with siblings and birth parents. Siblings may reside in foster care, a residential treatment setting, with relatives, or with birth parents. It is best if your child does not have to count her siblings among her losses. She will inevitably reestablish contact with them as soon as she is old enough to do this on her own, so it will be safer and healthier for the child if you help maintain and monitor the contact. Some, but not all, birth parents may be difficult to establish a relationship with. However, if the child has a bond with those parents, she will seek them out as soon as possible, just as she will her siblings and any other birth relatives. If she is forced to stop seeing them when placed in your home, she will be angry as well as grieving, and this combination can create a severe obstacle to letting go of the past.

Children from other countries may have existing relationships that no one mentions to you. It's important to ask the workers in the orphanage if there are relatives or parents with whom the child should maintain contact. You may have to do some detective work to find addresses and names, but this can be done if planned for ahead of adoption time.

Take your child to a massage therapist. The stress of grief can cause all kinds of physical problems such as chronic headaches and stomachaches. A professional massage therapist can help your child release the tension from his body without interfering with the grief process. Be aware, though, that massage can also release memories from past trauma. Be sure that the massage therapist is aware that this is a potential risk for your child and be sure to tell the child's psychologist or therapist that he is receiving massage therapy. It would be best if the therapist has some telephone contact with the massage therapist. You can ask the massage therapist to teach you some simple massage techniques, so you can use these with your child at home.

Remember that anniversaries can trigger grief. A child with a traumatic background will have many significant anniversaries, some that he will recall without difficulty, and others that will be repressed from memory. The latter is most likely when an event was experienced before the child was verbal. These may include memories of when he was first removed from the birth parent, left a favored caregiver, or last saw a beloved grandparent. Other anniversary responses may arise at the time of year when the child was physically brutalized or around a certain time each month when the birth parents were less functional. Most of these significant times will not be known to you. Make note of the patterns of acting out and the events that seem to coincide with them and give this information to your therapist so that she or he can determine if the problem behaviors are related to a specific pre-placement date or event.

CHAPTER 4

Aggressive or Sexually Intrusive Behaviors

There are many reasons why your child may exhibit aggressive or sexually intrusive behaviors. One of the most common is a past history of experiencing or witnessing these types of behaviors. A psychological condition, such as a conduct disorder, may also make it difficult for your child to accept boundaries and to control her impulses. Past physical, sexual, or emotional abuse may be a cause of psychological conditions, but there are a few instances where a condition develops for no apparent reason. For children who have been in foster care, it is more likely that atypical behavior is the result of past abuse, since these types of experiences generally lead to removing the child from his or her birth parents in the first place.

Fetal alcohol syndrome or attention deficit disorder can also reduce a child's ability to control her impulses. Although these conditions don't cause violent behavior, when combined with other serious factors they can increase the overall risk of aggression or sexual intrusiveness.

There is now some research showing that there is a difference between the expected brain structure and the actual brain structure of some people with pathologically aggressive behaviors (McBurnett 2000). This indicates that some people may be born with the tendency to be aggressive, although it does not prove that they cannot be treated successfully or that everyone who is born with this brain structure will be violent.

Common Psychological Diagnoses

Conduct disorder and oppositional defiant disorder are common diagnoses for children and teens who are physically or sexually aggressive or both. These diagnoses must be made by a mental health professional who is qualified to evaluate psychiatric conditions. Psychological testing can provide further insight into your child's behaviors and thinking. The kinds of behaviors they consider for this diagnosis are present before the age of ten years and must have existed for more than six months. Symptoms may include:

- Often bullying or threatening others

- Deliberate cruelty to other people or to animals

- Deliberately causing property damage

- Chronic violations of rules such as curfew

- Losing his temper more than once a week

- Arguing with adults more than four times a week

- Being frequently and easily angered

- Deliberately annoying people

- Telling lies

- Being in trouble at home, at school, and in the community

Your child does not have to have all of these symptoms in order to be considered for one of these diagnoses, but must exhibit several of them over a period of several months. If your child has been behaving well, then suddenly develops these behaviors, the professional will likely look for other causes.

If it is clear that your child's acting out re-creates his own past abuse, he may be diagnosed as having post-traumatic stress disorder (PTSD). A child with this condition may act out regularly or sporadically in response to an anxiety trigger. Except in this scenario, the child is the abusive person.

The symptoms of post-traumatic stress disorder are sometimes confused with the symptoms of conduct disorder or attention deficit disorder (Perry 1999). The child is misdiagnosed and therefore receives an intervention that will prove to be unsuccessful at stopping or altering the behaviors.

The symptoms that a professional will consider for a diagnosis of post-traumatic stress disorder include:

- Disturbing memories or flashbacks

- Repeated nightmares and dreams of death

- Avoiding reminders of the trauma

- Anxiety about reexperiencing the trauma

- Behavioral reenactment of the trauma

- Physical problems

- Lack of interest in activities

It's not uncommon for people to decide it doesn't matter why a child is acting violently or intrusively, it only matters that the behaviors stop. However, there are often multiple contributing factors that cannot be resolved until the full extent of the diagnosis is known and the appropriate treatments applied. For example, a child with oppositional defiant disorder and attention deficit disorder may not benefit from any kind of therapy until she receives medication to help control her attention problems. And play therapy can be very useful for a child who has post-traumatic stress disorder, but it is generally useless for a child who has a conduct disorder.

Sexually Intrusive Behavior

Most parents do not expect their child to behave in a sexual manner. The child who does has probably learned that sexual behavior is secretive, rather than private, and therefore has become adept at hiding what she is doing to others. Your child may be in your home for quite some time before you realize that this is going on. Sexual intrusiveness may occur with all of these other behaviors, or it may exist on its own. Sexually intrusive behavior can take many forms, including:

- Overtly aggressive sexual acts against another child or an animal

- Initiating sexual touch with a younger or less experienced child

- Trying to watch you dress or bathe

- Manipulating younger or less experienced children into sexual behaviors with each other, with an animal, or with an inanimate object

- Repeatedly displaying sexually provocative behaviors to children, adults, or both
- Purposefully dressing in a sexualized manner

Effect of Aggression or Sexual Intrusion

Most adoptive parents are not prepared for the changes a violent or sexually intrusive child will bring to their family. Parents generally adopt a child to fill their own need to parent and, perhaps, to make a positive contribution to the world. The pre-placement training that often occurs cannot prepare you for the experience of living with such a child.

Once your child is in the home, you may find that these types of behaviors are exhausting and frightening for the rest of the family (and for your child). It can mean that your family resorts to having locks on doors, alarms in certain rooms, and that you and your other children have to develop a sense of hypervigilant behavior that mirrors that of an abused person. In other words, the rest of the family may begin to feel victimized. This can result in problems in your marital relationship, your other children acting out because of the stress, and, in the worst cases, the eventual breakdown of your family or removal of the child. It can be devastating for you to realize how intense your own anger toward the child has become. The lack of rewards and the inability to ever trust the child can create an atmosphere of hostility in the home that pervades every encounter and every relationship.

Can My Child Recover?

Most children who show these types of behaviors early in the placement can resolve them with appropriate therapy, combined with the suggestions presented here. The behaviors can be extinguished in most children. The child who once killed the family rabbit can grow up to become a kind and sensitive adult. The key to surviving these behaviors with your family intact is to get an accurate understanding of what your child is doing, how long she or he has been doing it, what factors have led to the behaviors (past abuse, brain damage, or a psychiatric disorder) and then find the appropriate therapeutic and family interventions. In the following scenario, Dave and Molly struggle with the effect their seven-year-old son's behavior has on their household.

Life Lesson: Coping with Aggression

Dave and Molly were worried. Jennifer, their ten-year-old birth daughter, was beginning to have seizures every week. She had been born with cerebral palsy, and was paraplegic as well as mentally handicapped, so they were used to her frail health and high needs. Jennifer had never really developed language ability, but she had been a joy to them all of her life. Her cheerful personality and smiling face were a constant source of pleasure to all who knew her. She had had seizures when she was very young, but they had stopped several years ago. Now they were back, and Dave and Molly had begun to wonder if it had anything to do with the stress of having Yury in the home.

Yury was seven years old when Dave and Molly adopted him from Eastern Europe. They knew that there would be some challenges to face, but they were experienced adopters. Four years earlier, they had adopted six-year-old Alexandra from the same orphanage, and with the help of a good therapist, the child and family had adjusted easily. Alexandra was now ten years old and doing well in school, had lots of friends, and was horse crazy. But Yury was a different matter. He had been an angry little boy right from the start. The eager face and bright mind that he displayed in the orphanage had masked a tendency to violence that no one had warned them about. He had only been home three days when Dave discovered Yury beating the dog.

"Dog is dirty," Yury said in his heavily accented English. "Hate dogs."

"The dog is part of our family, Yury," Dave said. "In our family we take care of the pets." A month later, Dave and Molly reluctantly gave the dog away to some kindly looking strangers who answered their ad in the paper. There had been too many painful squeals and yips from behind closed doors, or out in the backyard, and they had finally acknowledged that they could not keep the dog safe from their new son. Jennifer and Alexandra had been heartbroken. Both had cried for nights after the people drove away with the dog.

It was not just the dog who suffered. The house was beginning to look like a war zone. In a fit of rage, Yury tore chunks of wallpaper off of his bedroom walls. Another time, when he had been sent to his room for hitting Alexandra, he had smashed a hole in the wallboard beside the bathroom door.

"I'll fix the hallway," Dave said, "but I'll be darned if I'll repair his room until I see some sign of change in that kid."

"You can't leave it like that," Molly replied. "The social worker who is doing the post-placement visit will think we treat him differently from the girls."

"We do treat him differently," Dave bristled, "because he behaves differently. They are nice, normal little girls. They play, they hug, we can talk to them, and read to them. He's not like that. Molly, I don't think this is going to work."

"Don't say that, Dave. He has his good times. And besides, you know it takes time to undo past hurts. He hasn't even been here six months. And he hasn't had any therapy. Please don't give up yet,' she begged.

The therapist they had used when Alexandra was adopted saw them once. "I'm sorry, but I'm not adequately trained for this type of problem," she said. "Alexandra had a lot of adjusting to do, but she was emotionally stable and didn't have any violent tendencies. Yury is not the type of child I generally work with, and I don't think I can do your family any service if I see him. You need to get him to someone who specializes in things like attachment disorder and violence."

So, Molly called up the community mental health center. They did not have anyone available who worked with attachment disorder, but they did have several therapists who worked with children who had been abused and who had witnessed violence. This sounded ideal for Yury, and Molly eagerly had Yury placed on the waiting list.

"It will be three to six months before someone can see him," the intake worker said.

"What can I do in the meantime?" Molly asked.

"I'm not allowed to give advice until you are actually clients," the worker replied. "But I can suggest you join a support group."

"Great. Where can I find one?"

"Well, I don't know of any going on at the moment. But I'll put your name on the list for people who want a support group and if I hear of one, I'll call you."

"Do you have a waiting list for people who are waiting to be called?" Molly asked dryly.

The weeks went by. Jennifer's seizures continued to occur weekly. Dave and Molly did all they could to protect her and Alexandra from their own anger and frustration with Yury, and they did their best to discipline him fairly and without raising their voices. They knew he must have had it very rough in the orphanage, and perhaps with his birth parents. He was such a beautiful little boy. His big eyes and open face convinced Molly that there was a loving child hidden under the rage. Dave and Molly were not quitters and they resolved to manage until the mental health people could begin working with them. They enlisted the aid of friends and family who were willing to give them breaks and take the girls, and sometimes Yury, on outings. But it was not enough. They were exhausted from the constant supervision Yury required, and from anticipating what he might destroy next or what might trigger his next rage. Molly knew she and Dave were bickering more frequently and lately Alexandra had been asking veiled questions about the stability of the marriage.

Night after night, Molly found she could not fall asleep. She yearned for the days when life had been easier. The pre-Yury days, as she had come to consider her life before they had adopted their son. Was this going to work? Was he salvageable? What if the doctor determined that it was the stress from having Yury in the home that was causing Jennifer's increased seizure activity? Would they have to sacrifice one child in order to save the other? To save the marriage?

Meeting the Challenge

There are ways for families to deal with aggressive and sexually intrusive behavior. The following pages offer tips and techniques to help you meet the challenge.

You must have dealt with your own past abuse issues. If you were abused in the past, it's crucial for you to resolve this issue prior to the placement. If this has not occurred, your child's acting-out behaviors will quickly become intolerable to you. If the placement occurs before you have found resolution, it's important that you enter therapy as soon as possible.

To either reduce or increase aggression, look at how your own personality interacts with that of your child. Do you easily get into power struggles with others at work? Do you yell at people? Do you have trouble keeping your temper? Are you easily targeted? Do you fall into a victim role readily? We all have personality traits that can either contribute to the increase or decrease of aggression. You cannot change who you are, but you can honestly explore how much your personality plays a part in either helping your child to heal or helping your child to stay entrenched in his aggression.

On a yearly basis, as long as symptoms persist, have your child undergo a thorough psychiatric or psychological assessment. Any underlying psychiatric conditions have to be considered so that the correct therapeutic approach can be determined. Medications may also be necessary if your child has other existing conditions, such as attention deficit disorder or an obsessive-compulsive disorder.

Continue with professional therapy for you and your child, as long as the behaviors persist. Aggressive and sexualized behaviors require ongoing professional intervention. You can use techniques at home that support the therapy, but they cannot provide the therapy themselves, nor can they create the desired change in the child without professional support. You also need the help of the therapist to learn how to deal with your own feelings about these types of negative behaviors, and to learn how to deal with the high level of stress that is the result of living with a violent or sexually intrusive child.

Make sure the child's therapist is trained in working with child and youth offenders. This is not the time to be using an inexperienced therapist, nor is it the time to be using one who focuses on the child's past victimization or excludes her current predatory behaviors.

Make sure that all of the professionals and service people involved with your child and family are communicating regularly and using similar approaches. If the service team members are in conflict or are suggesting drastically different approaches, then your child will feel like she is in charge of the adults (and actually, she will be) and will not make good progress. The professionals should be unified, they should have the same goals, and they should all be communicating with you.

Be prepared to have your child removed from the home when the behaviors are escalating. You may hesitate to have your child removed from your home, fearing you won't be able to get him back, or that your child will perceive removal as rejection. However, it's not safe to live with a child who is going through a cycle of severe, violent acting out. Family members are at risk of being harmed, and your emotionally vulnerable family members may be at risk. Escalating aggression or chronically intrusive behaviors are beyond the ability of a family to manage, so other living situations must be utilized. Remember, the structure and predictability of a therapeutic placement are often comforting for an overwhelmed or traumatized child. This setting is not a punishment. It's often an important step in fostering change. If the child cannot return home for the foreseeable future, you can still maintain an ongoing relationship with her and perhaps include her in significant family events such as birthdays and holidays.

If your therapist advises that you use physical restraint, get trained in the proper techniques. The use of physical restraint with severely aggressive or violent children is hotly debated by professionals. If you are working with a therapist who advises that you do so, there are some things to consider. First, check with your local child protection authorities to learn if they consider this to be child abuse. Child welfare standards should be the same throughout the country, but they are often interpreted differently by different agencies. Find out if you are at risk of losing the child if you use restraint.

If you are satisfied that your therapist is giving you the correct advice, and you have checked with the local child welfare authorities, then find someone who can train you how to do restraints safely. Physical restraint can result in injury to you or to your child if you do not do it properly. Call a local child care or family support agency to find out who is licensed to give this type of training in your area. It should be someone who is experienced in restraining children. A licensed trainer who only knows how to restrain adults and simply modifies the techniques for use with children is putting you and your child at risk for serious injury.

Have a written plan for when you will use this technique and do not vary from that plan. Make sure that you have created this plan with your therapist and the restraint trainer, so you are only using it when someone's safety is in immediate danger from the child.

Stay in charge. A child who has experienced abuse has often been placed in pseudo-adult roles and may expect to be the adult in the new family. She may be skilled at eroding parental authority and control, or may never have known an adult to assume those responsibilities. It is important to gently, but firmly and consistently, remind her that you are in charge and that you are the final authority on all decisions. A democratic family orientation can evolve over time, but will not likely be in the best interests of your child, until the emotional issues are resolved. Although your child may initially oppose your authority, children find security in reasonable and fair limits.

Use all of the techniques in chapter 2. These techniques are equally useful for children who are violent, sexual, or both. The "feet technique," points, time-out, and helping the child cope with social isolation are particularly useful.

Talk about boundaries. A boundary is a psychological protective bubble that surrounds each of us. It helps us to feel that we have enough individual space both physically and emotionally. Children who have been abused have often lost these bubbles and may not recognize them in others. You can help your child develop her own bubble, and learn to recognize those of others, by talking about them. For example, if she is sitting too close to a sibling, and you know this will lead to a fist fight, you can intervene early by stating, "Oh, Robbie. Look, you moved into David's bubble. Move over a bit, so you both have room for your bubbles." Or, "Kathy, I love cuddling with you, but you're sitting so close that my bubble is getting squished. Can you move over an inch, so both our bubbles have room?"

Always have a tape player with earphones and a handheld computer game in the car. Boredom and transitions are often triggers for sexual or aggressive behaviors. Let your child listen to favorite tapes while going to and from places to keep him distracted and occupied. The tapes will have to be changed frequently to keep him interested. Handheld games will also keep your child busy and are more suitable for teens. Buy the same tapes or games for the siblings.

Do not hit back. This sounds simple, but living with an aggressive or overtly sexualized child may eventually trigger an outburst in even the most sweet tempered of parents. This is best avoided by prevention. Get your child into respite (described later in this chapter), to a daycare, over to a grandparent's house, or somewhere else so that you get a break when the tension has been intense for a period of time. If you do hit your child, it's important that you take a breath, give yourself a time-out, and then face what happened openly with the child, the family, and the support services. Your child needs to see you take responsibility and implement measures to prevent it from happening again. If it does happen again, it's very important that you seek help to consider whether your child can safely remain in your home.

Teach your child about choices. When your child is aggressive or sexual, talk to her about what other behavior she could have used when she had the triggering feeling (anxiety, anger, irritation, boredom, arousal, etc.). She may try to wiggle and twiggle her way out of this conversation, but use a calm tone and a supportive demeanor, and run through the list of alternative behaviors each time a situation arises. Timing is crucial with this. At the beginning of the placement, it may be important to wait until things have settled down, but after your child knows the routine, this conversation should be held as soon as possible after an incident occurs. Be careful that you are in control of your feelings and are able to move beyond your own anger at whatever the child has just done.

Teach your child how to apologize. When it is appropriate, have your child face his victim, say what he has done wrong, and apologize. This is not easy. It may take months of practice before he is able to even look at his victim without laughing or spitting or hitting, but it is important to try to get to this point. Remember: Primary consideration must be given to the victim, and if she is not willing to participate, do not use this technique.

Model how to apologize. Children learn by mirroring adult behavior. When you make a mistake or a misjudgment, or overreact to a situation, it is important that you apologize appropriately for your behavior, so that your child can see you being accountable for your actions and acting in a responsible manner.

Protect the pets. Violent or sexually intrusive children may harm the family pet. Your child may do so in ways that do not leave marks and are not obvious to the rest of the family. With these children, it's best not to have any kind of household pet. However, if the animal was already in the home prior to the placement, make sure that the child is never alone with it.

Provide a separate bedroom. A child with sexual and aggression issues requires her own bedroom to ensure that she does not have an opportunity to terrorize the siblings or damage their belongings. Siblings should be allowed to have a lock on their door, and be assured that they have room in their home in which they do not have to cope with the violent or sexual behavior of the acting-out child.

Teach your child how to recognize, label, and cope with feelings. Frustration, boredom, disappointment, excitement, anticipation, anxiety, and fear are often the main triggers for acting-out behaviors. Both you and your child need to learn the early warning signs that he displays when he is experiencing an overwhelming emotion. Learn to label the feelings ("I feel angry") and then find a fast way to intercede, before the feelings escalate into negative behaviors. Many self-help books have pictures of faces that demonstrate the feelings and these pictures can be placed on the refrigerator or a bulletin board so your child can learn to identify the facial expression with the word or feeling. It's also helpful to learn to predict situations in which your child is likely to experience one of these feelings. Talk to him about it ahead of time. For example, "Ricky, we are going to the movies today, and we will have to wait in the line for a long time. You might feel bored while we're waiting. What toys do you want to take with you?"

If you have just returned from a long car trip and everyone is tired and crabby, be aware that these types of feelings can lead to violent or sexual behaviors, and take precautions before these happen. Talk to your child about it. For example: "Jill, I know you are excited and tired from going to the fair today. Sometimes when you have these feelings, you behave inappropriately. What can we do together to make certain this doesn't happen today?" It's not up to your child to devise a means of intercepting her own behaviors, but it may increase her motivation if she is included in the process. This also keeps the issue out in the open and makes everyone more careful. And don't relax your guard just because your child appears to be participating in the process.

Meet with teachers on a regular basis. You, your child, and his teacher should meet at least once a month to discuss how he is behaving and what strategies each party is finding most useful to prevent or resolve negative behaviors. You and the teacher should meet without your child for part of each meeting. Face-to-face meetings ensure that you are aware of what is happening at school and reduce your child's opportunity to make false allegations against the teacher, or even you.

Consider the impact of peer relationships and the school experience. At your regular school meetings, find out from the teacher whether your child has any friends and, if so, what kind of influence they have. Violent and sexually intrusive children are often socially ostracized and lonely, and this increases their stress, frustration, and rage. They may seek out peers who are functioning in equally negative ways, and this almost always leads to an increase of acting-out behaviors in the community. Or, your child may be so lonely that he is retreating into a fantasy world. This, too, often leads to increased acting out. It may be necessary to consider home schooling to reduce the child's daily stress.

This can be difficult for you when you need a break from your child, but it should be considered.

Place siblings and your acting-out child in different schools. Siblings will generally be embarrassed by the reputation your troubled child has in the school. Your child may also feel overwhelmed and ashamed of his inability to make friends or to get as good grades as the siblings. Attending separate schools allows siblings to have an environment where they are not subjected to an acting-out child, who can have an environment where he is not compared to his better-behaved siblings.

Include third parties. Aggressive and sexually intrusive children can be skilled at blaming others and presenting themselves as "victims" of "mean" parents. It's important to avoid this misrepresentation by including the third party in discussions. For example, if Grandma is starting to hint that you are too strict with Johnny, then you and Grandma need to sit down together and talk about how Grandma arrived at this belief. Once you and Grandma have thoroughly discussed this, then include Johnny. This can be done without blaming Johnny or accusing him of lying. Rather, the concerns and how Grandma and you have resolved them can be presented to Johnny.

Develop consequences for negative behavior. You need to consider how you will respond at the moment you catch your child in a negative scenario. For example, you may agree that he will be sent to his room and nothing more will happen until both parents have had an opportunity to calm down and discuss the event, or until the therapist has become involved, or until the police arrive. A child will often initiate an event to provoke you, so it's important that he learn very quickly that you will not respond in an equally violent, rageful, or hysterical manner, but rather a well-thought-out, calm manner.

Use respite care. A family cannot live with the daily stress of a violent or sexually intrusive child without taking a break. Make arrangements with the local social services to provide respite services from a licensed foster home that specializes in caring for children with this type of problem. It is also important that the siblings have a break from the stress, and have an opportunity to have quality time with you.

Join or create an appropriate support group. You need an outlet where you can vent your anger, frustration, and exhaustion without fear of being judged. You need to be able to say that you "hate" your child to people who understand that you love the child more than anything. This can only come from your peers.

Do not let your child rule your life. Your child can become the focus of all your attention and energy. It's crucial to your marriage and the stability of the family that you continue to have other interests and to maintain a social life. If you are afraid to go out because your aggressive teen will leave the house or burn it down while you are gone, you should go out anyway. Parents aren't prison guards, and are entitled to have their adult time away from the house.

Be firm in your rule that your child is not allowed to hurt you or anyone else. Do not hesitate to hold your child's arm if he is striking out, or to take away a stick or scissors if he is in an escalating mode. You must not become his victim. He will believe that if you cannot protect yourself, then you cannot protect him or stop him.

Be consistent. Stick with the rules you have made and don't back down. If he has been "good" all week, and then has one minor incident of violence, treat it the same as you would if he had been "bad" all week and the incident was more serious. You must have zero tolerance for violent or inappropriate behavior at all times.

Call the police if necessary. If the violence or sexual behavior is severe or cannot be contained, call the police. They can contain the child, remove her to a hospital, or at least calm the situation. Have a plan for what you will ask the police to do. And don't expect your child to become well behaved just because a police officer is present. Faced with an obvious authority figure, your child may become more aggressive.

If your child is removed by police, have a plan for when and how you will let her back in to the home. The hospital, or the emergency foster home, will not keep your child any longer than they have to, and will be pushing you to take her home as soon as possible. Make a contract with your child defining what your child will have to do before you take her home. This may include counseling, or it may include checking out a new medication with the psychiatrist. Your contract might specify that the other children in the home will have input in negotiating her return home. Whatever your contract is, enforce it, and do not take her home until you feel satisfied that all parts of the plan have been met.

Don't use any threat unless you intend to follow through with it. If you say it, then you'd better mean it. Threats should be presented as boundaries or limits. For example, "Jimmy, if you do that again, I'm calling the police" means that the next time Jimmy does it, you had better be prepared to call the police, or he will know that this is yet another barrier that he can cross without consequences. Also, if you don't follow through, his belief that you cannot be trusted will be reinforced .

Do not tolerate swearing, sexualized behavior, or violence from anyone in your family. Though much easier said than done, the child has to know your limits, and know that her adoptive home is safe *for* her and that it is safe *from* her. And she has to know that these behaviors are not acceptable when anyone does them. It is your job to constantly reinforce that your home cannot be changed by her. She will be doing her best to control you with her behavior and to re-create the violence of her past. Let her know that there are no degrees of bad language or degrees of sexually inappropriate behavior.

Clearly state family boundaries. If your child has sexualized behaviors, then everyone in the house must abide by the boundaries you set up. Your boundaries should specify that no one can be undressed in the same room as the child; robes must be worn over pajamas whenever family members are out of bed; no more than one person can be in the bathroom at a time; bedroom doors stay open if there are two children in the room; the other children can have locks on their doors; TV must be closely monitored; and sexualized shows are off-limits.

Seek professional help for the siblings. It is very difficult for siblings to live with the rigid boundaries and structure that is necessary to protect them from an offending child. A therapist can help the siblings to understand how to cope with the stress of their living situation and will provide them with a safe and appropriate arena for venting their feelings.

CHAPTER 5

Attention Deficit Hyperactivity Disorder

Attention deficit hyperactivity disorder (ADHD) and *Attention deficit disorder* (ADD) are some of the most commonly diagnosed behavior disorders of childhood. They are the diagnostic terms for a condition in which the child or adult is unable to maintain a reasonable attention span. When hyperactivity is involved, the person displays a seemingly uncontainable amount of energy, to the point that he interferes with people around him. Many people who have ADD as children still show the symptoms into adulthood.

ADD and ADHD are the result of neurological dysfunctions in the brain. Children with ADD and ADHD are not willfully bad. Scientific studies have shown that brain scans of children diagnosed with ADD/AFHD are measurably different from scans of children without the diagnosis. It is not yet understood what causes the condition, although it looks as if heredity is a factor in some children. Also, ADD/ADHD can result from prenatal exposure to alcohol, encephalitis, seizures, or head injury, to name just a few contributing conditions.

Psychiatrists have found that there are three types of attention deficit disorder: attention deficit/hyperactivity disorder predominantly inattentive type; attention deficit/hyperactivity disorder predominantly hyperactive-impulsive type; attention deficit/hyperactivity disorder combined type. In other words, the diagnoses are now separated into the categories of those who have hyperactivity, those who have only inattention, and those who have both hyperactivity and inattention.

Characteristics of ADD/ADHD

There are many characteristics common to the condition. The following are the most common and would be noticeable from early childhood. A child with ADD/ADHD would exhibit some, but not necessarily all, of the following behaviors. He may not be able to:

- Begin tasks
- Complete tasks
- Stay with tasks
- Focus or pay attention
- Organize work or play

Additionally, he may:

- Require supervision beyond what is developmentally normal
- Move and fidget constantly and excessively
- Be excessively active during sleep
- Have angry outbursts
- Be impulsive
- Be easily distracted
- Be disruptive everywhere: in class, social situations, and the home
- Be easily bored
- Be socially isolated
- Have memory impairment
- Be prone to accident and injury
- Run everywhere, climb on everything
- Be forgetful
- Constantly lose items such as jackets, school supplies, and completed assignments

The Impact of ADHD on Your Family

Attention deficit (with or without hyperactivity) presents behaviors that can wear out anyone. Siblings may become quickly frustrated, present an increased level of attention-seeking behavior, or reject the child. You may find that you can't leave your ADD child alone for a minute without some kind of problem arising. Constantly supervising your child can make you feel more like a prison guard than a parent.

The school system will likely demand a great deal of your time as the teachers wrestle with your child's behaviors. The school will expect you to be a highly contributing part of the educational team.

Your child's ADD/ADHD may affect your social life. You may find that you and your child are no longer welcome in the homes of friends due the disruptive and apparently disobedient behaviors of your child. Friends may refuse to come over because they cannot cope with the frenetic energy and the child's need for so much parental attention. The exhaustion and disruption to the home can lead to marital problems, siblings acting out in order to compete for attention, as well as chronic frustration and exhaustion for you. Jim and Kathy's story will help you understand how devastating ADD/ADHD can be for a family.

Life Lesson: The Demands of ADHD

Jim and Cathy were ecstatic when the call finally came. The social worker was proposing a little boy named Todd. He was barely two years old and had been in the same foster home since the age of six months. The foster mother and the social worker described Todd as "all boy" and "full of energy." The pre-placement visits went well. Todd was indeed full of energy, as foretold. In some ways, Cathy thought he might be a bit overly rambunctious. He seemed to flit from one toy to another; he broke something every time Cathy and Jim were in the foster home.

"It's just his way," said the very experienced foster mom. "When he gets his own family and settles down, he'll be fine."

The young social worker nodded in agreement. "We see this all the time," she said. "Even when these little tykes have been in the same home for a long time, they have a sense of not belonging, and it comes out in their behavior. With this energy level though, he's sure to be a sports enthusiast. I hope you're ready to coach some soccer, Jim."

Jim and Cathy had attended the extensive pre-adoption placement and they were aware that they could be seeing signs of ADHD. But the social worker and the foster mother both seemed to think it would be all right. Todd had been assessed by a team of pediatric specialists as being normal in all areas of development, even ahead of his age in a few. Best of all, there was no record of the mother drinking during her pregnancy. The available information was that she had been a young woman who smoked too much and was slightly underweight, but she had not been a drinker. She had been raised in foster care herself. Todd's father was unknown. Tragically, Todd's mother had contracted HIV and become too ill to care for her baby, so she had voluntarily placed the child for adoption and then disappeared. On the positive side for Todd, she was believed to have been a fairly good mom while she had him, so there was no reason to suspect any form of attachment disorder.

"This is too good to be true," Cathy said to Jim. "No fetal alcohol syndrome, no attachment disorder, and he's the most beautiful little boy I've ever seen. But what if he turns out to have attention deficit disorder?"

"Well, that isn't so bad. It's just ADD. They have drugs for that now, and at least it isn't fetal alcohol syndrome or any of the really bad stuff," Jim said. "He kind of looks like my Uncle Joseph, don't you think? That blond hair and the big wide eyes. Uncle Joseph was a good-looking guy in his day. Very athletic."

"Well, you'll have to ask your mom if he was as busy a little guy as our boy," Cathy replied, smiling. "Our boy, Jim. Our little boy."

For the first few days of the placement, Todd was quiet and withdrawn, but Jim and Cathy knew about grief and loss in adoptees, so they were patient and let the boy talk to his foster mother on the phone every night. At first, his grief was so thick they could almost touch it. Cathy's maternal instinct came on full force, as she cared for her sad little child. After a few days he began to brighten up. Soon, Todd was all over the place, his energy level back to normal.

Cathy quit her job to be a full-time mom. She looked forward to taking Todd to parent and tot swimming, and to gym classes. But she soon found herself easily frustrated by his behaviors. He could not stay still long enough to learn to hold his breath in the water. Several times, he managed to twist out of Cathy's arms and sink straight to the bottom before she could grab him. Gym was even worse. He ran all over the place, stepping on the other children, and trying to climb straight up the ropes that went up the side of the gym wall. The instructors in both places started to pay less and less attention to Todd and Cathy. Even the other parents were beginning to give them a wide berth for fear that Todd would grab or hit one of their children. Finally, Cathy stopped going to structured events with Todd. It was not worth the effort.

"We have to do something, Jim. I can't stand this any longer. I can't get anything done in the house, because I have to watch him every minute. I can't go out to get a break because no one will baby-sit for me. I can't even work in the yard because he starts pulling out all the plants I put in, or he runs off down the street. He can open the gate even after you put the childproof lock on it. Is it just me? Am I failure? What if I wasn't meant to be a mother?" Cathy asked tearfully.

"Look," said Jim. "In our hearts we knew this was not just a lot of energy, and we might as well admit it; he has all the symptoms of ADHD. Why don't you get a referral to a specialist and get him on some medication? That will fix things and then you can get on with enjoying him. And maybe we can think of applying for another child."

Cathy looked at Jim for a moment before answering. "I'll take him to the doctor, but I'm not ready for another child. He takes everything I have." Cathy was hesitating, trying to keep the resentment out of her voice. "You aren't with him all day. You leave at eight and get home at six. He goes to bed at eight, or at least he goes to his room. All you have to do is bathe him and roughhouse awhile, then put him back to bed a few times. I can't manage Todd and another child, Jim, especially not another child that might have a special need."

"Todd doesn't have any special needs," Jim bristled. "He probably just has ADHD. And don't say I don't do my part. We agreed that you would stay home and I would work. And I do my bit on the weekends and in the evenings. You're always so tired. I do the laundry most of the time, and I do the yard work, and I vacuum and I cook on weekends. I take Todd to my mom's on Sundays so you can sleep during the morning and have part of the afternoon to yourself."

Cathy was quiet. Jim did do his part. But he wasn't there during the day, and he really couldn't understand how frustrating and exhausting it was. Todd was thriving in their home, and as a result, he was growing quickly. That meant it was getting harder and harder to find an outlet for his roaming attention and his impulsive, destructive acts. Cathy secretly wished she could go back to work. But Jim would be disappointed if she did that. He made a good salary and they didn't need the money. Jim was proud of being able to support a traditional family, and he valued Cathy's role as a stay-at-home mom. She didn't want to let Jim down. She made the appointment with the specialist.

The specialist confirmed attention deficit disorder. But she wouldn't give Todd any medication.

"Why not?" asked Jim. "At the training, they talked about how effective the drugs are. I thought it was standard procedure."

Cathy sighed. "She won't prescribe medications for a child this young. She said there aren't enough reliable studies to show the long-term effects of medicating a child Todd's age. And she said that he will need it when he starts school, so that is soon enough. She talked a lot about the impact of medical intervention on the developing brain, but I didn't understand it." Cathy hoped Jim didn't pick up on her lie. Of course she had understood what the doctor said. But she hadn't liked it, and she didn't have the energy to go through it all with Jim. He could look it up himself on the Internet. To her, the thought of three more years with Todd's behavior was like a prison sentence, and she was fearful about how she would get through those years.

However, Cathy did get through the next three years. Todd continued to grow rapidly and in full health. His speech developed quickly, and it was obvious to everyone that he was a very bright little boy. There were moments with Todd that were pure joy. Cathy cherished them. But most of her days were spent in an exhausting round of chasing after him, watching him, trying to think ahead of him, cleaning up from his destruction, and dealing with her own loneliness. She had lost her work friends when she left the office to stay home. Todd's behavior soon made friends unlikely in the environments where she would most likely meet other stay-at-home moms. Finally, the time came for Todd to start kindergarten and medication.

Cathy took Todd back to the specialist, who was willing to provide a prescription, this time. Cathy listened as the pharmacist explained the dosage, then asked, "But that's only good for part of the day. It'll wear off by the afternoon. And what about the weekends?"

The pharmacist shrugged. "I hear that from a lot of parents," he replied. "This is the standard dosage. It helps the child cope at school, but I guess it doesn't do much for the parents."

Cathy was near tears as she drove home. She loved Todd with all her heart. But she did not know how she would continue to cope with his behavior. The specialist had acknowledged that Todd had a serious case of ADHD, but when Cathy telephoned her, she would not budge on the dosage. That night, after Cathy put Todd to bed for the sixth time and picked up the pieces of the second lamp he had broken that day, she made up her mind. She was going back to work. It didn't matter what Jim said, she would put Todd in after-school care, and she would have the day free from his excessive activity. Lately, Jim had been hinting that it was time to apply to adopt another child. "No," Cathy thought, "no more children." She would not be sentenced to staying home after school with Todd, and she would not subject a baby or toddler to Todd's impulsive and unpredictable behavior. Jim would be hurt and angry. It might even cause trouble in her marriage. "How much worse could it get?" she wondered. Cathy knew she had been emotionally withdrawing from Todd for a long time. She still loved him fiercely, but she did not like him much anymore. She had to steel herself every time he came into the room. And she had been withdrawing from Jim as well. His inability to understand her fears about having another child in the home had created a breach between them that she knew would only grow when she told him of her decision. This was not the family of their dreams. It never would be. Now she was beginning to fear that they might not make it as a family at all. As she finally drifted off to sleep that night, Cathy recalled Jim's words when they had first met Todd, "It's just ADD. How bad can that be?"

Overcoming the ADD/ADHD Challenges

There are a variety of techniques you can employ to help your child and your family cope with ADD or ADHD. Medication is helpful in many cases, but there are techniques that help your child learn how to better manage his behavior.

Consider medication. There are differing opinions on the value of medicating children. However, before ruling it out, you should at least consider whether it could allow your child to have a more successful home and school experience. Make sure that the pediatrician assessing your child's need for medication is well trained in ADD/ADHD and considers the viability of *not* medicating.

Use the specified tips for managing children with fetal alcohol syndrome. Chapter 6 offers techniques for dealing with fetal alcohol syndrome. Many children who have FAS also have ADD, so most of the techniques work with both groups of children.

Use dietary management. Do some experimenting. Find out which foods cause an increase in your child's energy. Not all children increase activity with sugar and dyes.

Try a variety of behavior-management techniques. Some techniques will work for a while, then stop being effective. That's a sign that it's time to switch to something else. But just because something stopped working a year ago, does not mean it cannot be tried again.

Use appropriate therapy. Many of the therapies commonly used with children, such as play therapy and nondirected talk therapy, are not effective with this condition. Behavior modification, cognitive behavioral therapy (CBT), biofeedback, and relaxation training can be effective for some children and youth with ADD/ADHD. You may also benefit from stress management counseling for yourself.

Drop an issue and return to it later. When your child cannot focus on a task or will not cooperate, leave it and return to it later. Over time, she may develop her own strategies for lengthening her attention span. However, while she is young, it is likely that when she *appears* finished, she really *is* finished and needs to move on. Respect this. Later, guide the child back to the task. Chores, such as cleaning the bedroom, can be broken into small tasks that are undertaken throughout the day. For example, have her pick up clothes from the floor every day after school, before play time; have her pick up her books and crayons from her bedroom floor or around the house every day, just before supper; have her pick up toys right before bed. While this method will never result in a completely clean room, it will at least mean that parts of the cleaning are done each day so that neither the child nor you is overwhelmed by a mess. It also allows her to see that she is able to contribute toward organizing her own life.

Do not engage in long explanations. Children and youth who have attention problems often also have coexisting memory problems (or they easily forget what they have been told because they cannot stay focused enough to listen). When something needs to be explained, do it in as few words as possible. Keep the explanation basic and short. If the issue is complicated, try explaining it over a period of time. Give the first part of the explanation in the morning, some more at lunch, and the rest after school. And remember to re-explain frequently.

Target the most difficult points of the day. Make note of which parts of the day or week are the most difficult for your child and plan around them. If he is always a problem right after school, make sure that this is never the time you take him grocery shopping or to a doctor's appointment. If he has problems on Fridays, then this is a good day for the family to go to the local swimming pool or to undertake some other activity that involves extensive use of the body's larger muscles. If he is always scattered and has had serious problems at school for the last two months of the year (nine or ten months of school is too long for most children with ADHD), then try to work out an agreement with the school so that he only attends it four days a week. He will likely be suspended a great deal in those last two months of school anyway, and a proactive approach to this problem can give him a better school record.

Assign chores that are short and have an obvious beginning and ending. The child with ADD/ADHD can manage her share of the chores just as well as the other children in the family. However, she will most likely complete only chores that can be done quickly and which have a clear finish. For example, emptying the dishwasher will only take a few minutes and she can see the progress as she takes out the dishes. Sweeping a floor is not as likely to succeed, because it is too easy to miss spots and to ignore major parts of the floor.

Negotiate a reduced homework load. Try to negotiate with the teacher for a reduced homework load. Your child or teen will have trouble focusing by the end of the day; too much homework requiring parental supervision can set the stage for intense daily parent/child conflict. If the homework load cannot be reduced, try to break it up into smaller time chunks. Your child can do one part right after school and another right after supper.

Enroll your child in sports that use the body's large muscle groups. Swimming is excellent because it uses the large muscle groups and leads to sports as a recreational activity, such as Friday night swimming. Sports that require intense concentration or complicated team work may not be fitting for children with ADD/ADHD since the kids may become frustrated with the rules, causing conflict with their teammates.

Teach your child about the condition. Your child needs to understand what it means to have ADD or ADHD, how it impacts his life, and how he can learn to manage it. This will help him to take control of his own symptoms and to become responsible for his behavior.

Give lots of encouragement. Your child will hear enough criticism, so make sure she also feels encouraged as she goes through the day.

Avoid overstimulation when possible. If you know that he cannot tolerate a grocery store with all the people and all the things he likes to touch, then don't take him shopping when you don't have to. As he gets older, there will be time and opportunity to teach him how to manage his behavior despite distractions. Right now, this is low on the list of priorities.

Teach your child how to cope with overstimulation in situations where it cannot be avoided. There will be situations that are impossible to avoid (family weddings, school events, shopping, etc.). Find something that can help your child to focus at such events, and teach him how to do this. For example, you can take a handheld video game for him to play when his attention jumps and his energy escalates. He can learn to play with the game as a means of rechanneling his thoughts and energy and of temporarily shutting out the overwhelming input coming from his environment.

Teach your child how to stop, think, and plan. Since impulse control is a major issue, teach him to stop, think, and plan. While he is growing up, you will have to be the person who tells him to stop, then helps him to consider what is going on around him, to look at what others are doing, and then to plan what he can do that will not make everyone mad at him. This takes a year or two to become a successful habit, but the payoff is worth the time.

Teach your child how to make lists. He can learn to write out, or to use symbols for, daily activities, chores, or reminders of what he has to do. This is likely something that he will have to rely on all of his life. Starting young can ingrain the habit. He can carry the list in his pocket, put it on the fridge door, or on the mirror in his bedroom. He can make the list each morning, or he can make a list for the next day before he goes to bed each evening.

Teach your child how to prioritize. Your child with ADHD cannot determine what is important and what is not. Help him to consider what needs to be done right away versus what can be done later.

Help your child learn to expand his attention span. Your child will have difficulty staying with one task from beginning to end. For example, he may repeatedly jump up from the dinner table to phone a friend, watch TV, or play with the dog. Each time he does this, bring him back to the table immediately, and have him resume his meal. No matter how tired you are, don't make exceptions. And do this with a friendly tone of voice.

Understand that your child's mood fluctuates. The mood fluctuations may be from medication or from environmental stimulation, but his mood can drastically change within seconds. Help him to refocus on the task at hand, or redirect him to do something that will not create frustration for him, letting his mood pass.

Teach your child to use others to help monitor his behavior. Your child cannot monitor his own behavior, but he *can* learn to watch other people to see how they are reacting to him. Teach him to notice when his friends are trying to stop playing, whether or not the teacher is starting to look mad, or if the neighbors are yelling at him. These are his cues that he has escalated to the point where he has bothered others. He can learn to use these as signals that it is now time to slow down and refocus. This process of noticing and responding will take several years to learn, but when used successfully will continue to be useful into his adult years.

CHAPTER 6

Fetal Alcohol Syndrome

Fetal alcohol syndrome (FAS) and partial fetal alcohol syndrome (also known as "fetal alcohol effects") are commonly used terms for the neurological damage that results when an embryo or fetus is exposed to alcohol. The effect of alcohol on the brain of the fetus occurs on a continuum from mild to severe. Different factors, such as whether the mother had proper nutrition or took drugs while pregnant, can interact to cause differing degrees of dysfunction. The damage to the brain is lifelong and can cause mental retardation, growth deficiencies, problems with the central nervous system, facial abnormalities, and behavioral and learning challenges. The most typical problems that adoptive parents deal with are learning disorders and behavioral disorders.

While FAS is the most preventable type of mental retardation, it nonetheless occurs in approximately one in 500 births. Partial fetal alcohol syndrome is not as easy to diagnose, but is thought to occur in approximately one in thirty births. In communities with an unusually high rate of alcoholism, the rate can even be as high as one in five births. However, it can be very common in older-child adoption because the families who are drinking throughout pregnancy often continue to have problems that interfere with good parenting; therefore, their children end up needing a different family than the one in which they were born.

Characteristics of FAS

There are a large number of characteristics associated with FAS. Not all children who have been prenatally exposed will have all of the symptoms, nor will they have the same degree of each symptom. In other words, a diagnosis of FAS or partial FAS can tell a prospective parent that there will be problems, but it will not tell the parent exactly what or how severe the problems will be. The following is a broad list of symptoms; however, it is unlikely that a child will have all of them:

- Reduced intellectual function
- Learning disabilities
- Poor impulse control
- Inability to relate behavior to consequences
- Poor short term memory
- Inconsistent knowledge base
- Difficulty grasping abstract concepts
- Sleep disorders
- Poor judgment
- Diminished capacity for personal empathy
- Rigid thought patterns (stubbornness)
- Depression
- Attention deficit disorder
- Inability to manage anger
- Physical problems, such as height and weight concerns (too small)
- Precocious puberty
- Seizure disorder
- Facial deformities
- Cardiac complications

These characteristics can be made even more complicated by other factors, such as early neglect or abuse. Furthermore, FAS could lead to your child becoming involved with drugs and alcohol, or becoming involved with the judicial system as the result of criminal activity (because they generally get caught). For some teens, the lack of impulse control and inability to foresee consequences can lead to early and repeated pregnancies, inability to get or keep a job, and inability to maintain an independent living situation as an adult. The learning disorders can lead to the youth being undereducated and unprepared for today's job market.

The Long-Term Outcome for Your Child

Today, the long-term outcome for a child with FAS is much different than it was in the past. Now, it is possible to get an early diagnosis and to begin appropriate intervention early on. Early diagnosis will not mend damage to the brain. It can, however, prevent secondary problems from developing and can diminish many of the negative characteristics so that they do not become an impossible challenge for either the child or for you.

Children with FAS and partial FAS do have some positive characteristics that make them easy to love. Some of these positive characteristics include:

- Tendency to be very affectionate and loving
- Tendency to forgive others for not understanding them
- Willingness to continue trying in spite of the odds
- Good sense of humor
- Willingness to try new things
- Tendency to be cheerful

The Impact of FAS on Your Family

FAS presents challenges that exhaust most families which do not have appropriate support. When an older child with FAS is placed in a home, there are generally several complicating factors. For example, the child may have a background that includes sexual or physical abuse. The addition of trauma to the diagnosis of FAS increases the risk that your child will display acting-out behaviors. Multiple residential moves prior to placement into your home may have decreased your child's ability to adequately develop attachment.

Some children with FAS are very superficially engaging, so they appear to adapt well and seem bonded. Within a very short time, however, you will discover that your child is not experiencing warmth and bonding at any meaningful level. Rather, he is as friendly and bonded to the mailman as he is to you. This can lead to severe disappointment for you, as well as a feeling that you have been tricked or betrayed by your child. Then, you may pull back emotionally and the placement becomes at risk for disruption. The following account of June's decision to adopt a child with FAS illustrates some of the challenges of dealing with this condition.

Life Lesson: Dealing with FAS

June, a single parent, fell in love with the picture in the photo listing. Mary-Beth was an adorable eight-year-old child. She wore glasses just like June had, before she was old enough for contact lenses, and Mary-Beth had thick brown hair that curled naturally at her shoulders. She had a charming smile and two crooked eyeteeth that could easily be fixed with braces. True, there was a diagnosis of partial FAS and a history of multiple moves, so June wanted to meet the child before making a decision. She knew she was capable of dealing with many challenges, and her years as a pediatric nurse had helped her to understand the challenges of raising older children. She also knew about the supports that were available.

Mary-Beth was charming and engaging. She was articulate and had a great sense of humor. The boundary issues so common to children with FAS did not seem to be present either. Mary-Beth had been with the current foster parents for almost eight months and they had not had any problems with her stealing, just a few lies and some forgetfulness. Nothing more. June decided to proceed to the next step and have Mary-Beth visit her home for a weekend. It went well. The two of them had lots in common and both wanted to get onto becoming a family as soon as possible. Mary-Beth moved in the last week of summer. The first few weeks went fairly smoothly. There were the minor adjustment problems that June had expected, and some disregard of rules. But, all in all, things were going well enough that June decided to apply to have the adoption finalized.

However, by Christmas break, June was starting to have some doubts. Mary-Beth had been caught stealing at school several times. She didn't take anything big, just candies or bus tokens from the other children. Although she cried, and swore never to do it again, the complaints from the school continued. Recently, Mary-Beth had been caught trying to steal a chocolate bar from the corner store. She had put it in her pocket while June was buying milk. To make matters worse, Mary-Beth was destroying her room piece by piece. June had dreamed of having a daughter for years, and when Mary-Beth moved in they had picked out the furniture together and made it into something any little girl would love. But Mary-Beth had picked at the wallpaper border beside her bed until it was half off. She had jumped on her bed so many times that the frame had broken. Most of the toys were broken, and pieces to all of the games were lost. The dolls were all missing an arm or leg. Some were missing their head; Mary-Beth had even cut the hair off of every Barbie.

The tutor June had hired was not working out either. He had repeatedly expressed his frustration at Mary-Beth's inability to remember what he knew she had learned the day before, and he was making sounds about quitting. This would be a problem, because the school did not have the resources to give Mary-Beth the extra help she needed since most of the school's learning-assistance budget went to children who were either physically or cognitively impaired. Mary-Beth's normal IQ meant that she could only get half an hour a day of extra help, and that was not going to be enough. The final straw for June had come when she realized that Mary-Beth was gradually picking off the expensive braces recently put on by the orthodontist. Bits of her tooth enamel had come off with the braces, so her back teeth had extensive damage. The fact that it hadn't seemed to hurt Mary-Beth had left the orthodontist flabbergasted. It was obvious that he suspected June of being highly inattentive to or even downright neglectful of her daughter.

June was beginning to question the decision to adopt Mary-Beth. It was obvious that she was in over her head. She was tired all the time, and she was getting so many calls at work from the school, that she had received a warning from her supervisor. And the support systems she had joined were not able to give her answers. All of the parents who attended the FAS support group were as frustrated and helpless as June. Actually, joining the support group had only made it worse, as June listened to the horror stories from the parents of teens with FAS. Most of the boys had been in trouble with the law. Several of the girls had babies. Most of them were using drugs or alcohol. None of them was succeeding in school and most had dropped out by eleventh grade. June dreaded the adolescent stage that was soon to come.

Still, June wasn't ready to stop the adoption proceedings. She had become bonded to Mary-Beth, although she was not sure Mary-Beth had actually bonded in return. And, when she wasn't angry or frustrated to the point of tears, June often found Mary-Beth to be a sweet and lovable little girl. The child had a wonderful sense of humor; she was attentive and caring to smaller children in the neighborhood; and she loved to cuddle with June and watch videos on Friday nights. June knew that if she let Mary-Beth go back into the foster care system, the child could not possibly understand what she had done to deserve this rejection. June knew she could not live with the guilt. With a knot in her stomach and her teeth gritted into a false smile, June signed on the dotted line. Mary-Beth became her daughter.

Overcoming the Challenge of FAS

Do not take the behaviors personally. A child who has severe FAS may steal from you, lie to you, and sneak around behind your back. You will have to accept these behaviors as part of the package and work toward long-term change. This can only be done when you clearly understand that the child is not doing these things *to* you. He is simply getting through his day in the way in which his mind allows him. He is not actively trying to harm you or destroy your relationship with him. In fact, the kind of plotting and planning that it would take for your child to deliberately trick or betray you is something of which the child with FAS is incapable.

Use most of the techniques from the attachment and aggression sections. These techniques continue to be useful when adapted for children with FAS. Many children with this diagnosis also have attachment challenges that are confused with other symptoms.

Establish predictable routines. Keep a calendar on the wall with daily events noted so your child can check what is happening next and perhaps begin to see patterns in the week.

Do not debate the rules. It is important to go over the reasons for rules from time to time, so that she understands they are for safety, consideration of others, or because they are common practice in this culture. But do not argue or defend the rules at times of conflict. Stay focused on the current issue and on how it needs to be resolved.

Keep your child's space or bedroom tidy. Your child should be learning how to keep her room tidy, but she may need extra help from you. It is important that she have a "clutter free" space in her life so that she can go there when she is overstimulated or upset and be in an environment that does not trigger more overstimulation.

Reinforce time concepts. Find a variety of ways to reinforce time. You can have large digital clocks in several areas, including on her bedroom wall, the kitchen, and the bathroom. Also, she can wear a watch. The clocks are important to help her understand that time passes and that the same moment cannot be used over and over again. Show her time changing, and remark how long it took you to cook supper, how long her television show is, or what time it was when she left school, then arrived home.

Use rewards rather than punishment. There is no point in punishing someone for having brain damage. Therefore, use rewards to create a more positive atmosphere and willing participation.

Change rewards frequently. To keep your child's interest in the rewards, change them frequently and make sure they are immediate.

Teach boundaries. This was explained in the section on aggression and is highly relevant to children with FAS and other organic brain disorders.

Keep explanations short and to the point. Do not bother with lectures. They do not work with any children. Say it once, demonstrate it once or twice, and then move on.

Break down chores into small tasks. Undefined, multiple tasks will become confusing for the child. Instead of saying, "Clean your room," say, "Pick up all the shirts from the floor and put them in the laundry basket." When that is done, say, "Pick up all the socks and put them in the laundry basket." However, be realistic. If there are more than one or two objects to be picked up, it is unlikely that your child's distractibility will allow her to finish the task without supervision.

Redirect and intervene. It is important to stay one step ahead and to redirect your child or intervene before problems arise. The pattern of problem situations will become apparent shortly after the placement. You will soon learn what you have to watch for.

Teach relaxation techniques. Your child can manage some of his behaviors with simple relaxation techniques for those times when he is overstimulated. There are many books available to teach you. Then, you can teach the child those that seem most suitable to his age and abilities.

Use the services of an occupational therapist or a professional skilled in sensory and/or auditory integration therapy. Standard counseling or therapy will not alleviate the symptoms of FAS or other forms of brain damage. However, occupational therapy, physical therapy, or medically based therapies that focus on the physical aspects of the condition can be extremely useful for children whose central nervous system is either over- or underfunctioning.

Have your child undergo a thorough medical and psychiatric exam regularly. Some children who have multiple diagnoses (such as FAS and ADHD) may be helped if the ADHD can be modified by medication. The benefits of medication may change with your child's age, so it is important to keep current with this.

Focus on social skills and living skills. These are as difficult for your child as academic skills, and require the same teaching and reteaching in order to prevent him from becoming lonely and isolated.

Help your child with transitions. Going from one activity to another, one place to another, one class to another, or one routine to another may be difficult for your child. Always give as much advance warning as possible for any potential change. A large calendar on the wall (separate from the daily events already mentioned) that indicates not only family routines, but school routines, can be helpful. Begin the day with a short discussion of what is expected to happen during the day, and warn your child of any potential changes to the routine.

Attend seminars and conferences on the topic. The knowledge of how best to support children and adults with FAS is changing rapidly. It is important to keep up with the newest interventions. Many conferences now include the children and youth. This is highly empowering and supportive for them.

Be actively involved in your child's school day. Develop a cooperative relationship with the school system so that issues that cross over between school and home can be dealt with in a consistent manner.

Develop advocacy skills. School systems and social settings do not accommodate children with organically based behavior disorders, such as FAS. The teacher, principal, Scout leader, swim teacher, and others may understand that the child has FAS, but will not likely put up with the apparent defiance and consistent breaking of rules for long. Just as you have to constantly teach and reteach your child, you will also have to constantly teach and reteach others who are involved in his life.

Teach the child to substitute tracking for memory. Memory is often impaired in children who were prenatally exposed to alcohol. Therefore, teaching him how to track his day may support or enhance memory. Tracking is done by recalling the events of the last hour (eventually expanded to the last day) by beginning with "What clothes were you wearing?" "What shoes were on your feet?" "Where did you go?" "Who did you talk to first?" "What did you talk about?" "Then who did you see?" Have your child touch his fingers as he does this, as if he were counting each memory. The conversation does not have to be stilted and artificial, but it does have to be led by you, and focused on helping him to describe, in sequence, what happened over a specific period of time. After a few months, or years, of regular practice with the technique, he will generally transfer this skill to other situations requiring sequential recall.

Say something positive to your child at least once every day. This will help both you and your child to remember that she is loved. It will also help you gain perspective, on days when it is difficult to feel the love for your child.

Be aware that some of the symptoms can be modified, but none will ever go away. These are lifelong problems. You may have to provide emotional, and perhaps financial, support to your child, even when he is an adult. This may include helping him to parent his own children, helping him to find and maintain a living situation, and helping him to get through life in general.

Plan for overstimulation. Children and youth with FAS may be easily overstimulated. When this occurs, have a pre-existing plan for dealing with the consequent behaviors. For example, the two weeks before Christmas are often a problem because the normal routine is varied at home and at school, and the excitement of the holidays can increase overactive and noncompliant behaviors. To counter this, find activities that will dissipate some of the energy. You may decide to go to the local recreation center for a swim each night. This allows your child to yell without being told to be quiet, facilitates the use of large muscle groups, and gets the child tired.

Avoid going to restaurants or public places where the child will have to behave during overstimulating times. If there is something different or more exciting than ususal happening that day, stay home as much as possible, or at least avoid places where your child will have to contain his behavior. For example, Halloween is not the night to go out for dinner. You know that your child will be excited from the events at school and anticipating getting more candy in the evening, so taking him to a public place is a setup for bad behavior.

Teach the child how to make choices. Children with FAS rarely make a thought-out, reasoned choice. Most of what you might consider to be a choice is actually an automatic response from your child. To teach choice, show him an apple and an orange, then ask him which he likes best, why he likes it, and what the differences are between the two. Show him two shirts and ask the same questions. Show him two toy cars and ask the same. Look at two computer games and ask the same. This can be done informally when helping him dress in the morning, at snack time, or at playtime. This should be done over a period of years, so your child can learn to consider different factors in order to come to a decision.

Go over the same information many times. Poor memory is one of the characteristics of FAS, so you will have to constantly reteach and re-train your child as she grows up.

Have your child get his things ready for school the evening before. The disorganized thinking can create havoc in the morning routine, and this, in turn, creates a crabby child and an equally crabby mom or dad. Help the child to learn what to get ready: jeans, shoes, socks, T-shirt, jacket, books, backpack. This also helps him to learn a routine and how to plan.

Review expectations and consequences regularly. Each day, your child will forget most of the rules of life, so he needs to be reminded gently and ahead of time. For example, several times a week, before school, remind her that if she yells out in class, she will be sent from the room. Or, you can remind her that she must come straight home from school, or you will begin walking with her (a dire threat to a thirteen-year-old).

Teach self-talk. Self-talk is exactly what it sounds like. It's the child talking about what she must do next, or where she must go, or how to do something. It is helpful in keeping her focused on the task at hand.

Link behavior to feelings. When she is in trouble, ask her how she feels. Does she feel sad? Mad? Upset? Confused? How does she think the person who is mad at her feels? When she is having a good time, ask the same. Does she feel happy? Excited? How does she think the person she is playing with feels? She needs help to connect behavior with feelings, so she can begin to understand consequences of her behavior, to self and others.

Role-play challenging situations with your child. There are many social situations in which your child may not understand the basic rules of behavior, as well as age-appropriate expectations. When you know one of these situations is coming up, run through the scenario with him and help him practice how to behave.

You can also do this for situations in which the child is generally in trouble that he did not cause. For instance, if you know that he is going to get picked on at school, teach him how to ask the teacher for help in an effective manner. Then role-play the scenario with him so that he can practice it enough times to remember what to do.

Plan for your child to take longer to grow up. It's not likely that your child will become independent of you as early as children who do not have FAS. He may need to live with you until his early to mid-twenties. He may need to keep moving out and back in until he is in his thirties.

You may have to plan to build or buy a house with a garage apartment or basement suite, so he can live close to you while he learns to be more independent. You may have to work past the age when you had intended to retire, because your older child with FAS genuinely requires your financial support into adulthood.

CHAPTER 7

Family Identity Formation

Do you remember your own teen years? Can you recall how you spent endless hours in front of the mirror, trying to decide if your hair was the right color or being upset at the size, shape, and position of your nose? Remember how important it was to wear the cool clothes, to like the same music as your friends, to hate the music that your parents listened to? Do you remember how determined you were to grow up and be different from your parents? Maybe you wanted to travel more than they did, or maybe you wanted to have more education, or live in an exciting city instead of a dull, small town. If there were serious problems in your family, maybe you were determined to drink less than your mom, or be home more than your dad. Whatever you found important at the time, you used your family and how they presented themselves to each other and to the world, as the springboard to the life you created as an adult. Your own identity was formed and transformed within the context of your family identity.

During the teens and early twenties, the search is on for an identity that is separate from the parents—unique to the individual, yet similar enough to some segments of society that the youth is able to establish friends and create her own family. Countless books and movies have been made about the search for identity, and major philosophical and psychological debates and studies have explored identity formation. For most people, the springboard for the establishment of an individual identity is the greater sense of family identity. And that is something that can be difficult to establish, when you adopt an older child.

What Makes It So Difficult?

You may find that the creation of a healthy sense of family identity can be complicated by myriad challenges. For many older children, the emotional and genetic ties to the family of origin are a challenge to the establishment of new bonds with the adoptive family. For others, a history of moves from one home to another has resulted in the child learning that it is too painful to allow himself to feel that he is part of any particular family. He learns, instead, to live like a boarder rather than an integral part of the family. When you begin to put pressure on him to become closer, or to make an emotional commitment to the group, he feels threatened and pulls away or acts out.

A sense of family identity can also be difficult to attain if your child felt abandoned by her original family or felt stolen from the original family. Unrelenting fantasies about reuniting with the birth mom, or unexpressed grief at being separated from the last foster parents, may prevent the new adoptee from establishing an identity as part of your family. Older children who are suffering from low self-esteem or unresolved past trauma may not feel that they are entitled to be included in the family identity that you are offering.

Children who have a diagnosis of ADHD, oppositional-defiant disorder, FAS, conduct disorder, or other disruptive behavior disorders, are at risk of failing to develop a sense of belonging to any healthy, positive group. Children who have these challenges may have a very good sense of what they need or want in life, but are unable to perceive how their needs affect others or to understand that others have needs as well. Therefore, your need to have the child function as part of the family may never be important to the child. She may also fail to integrate social roles; and she may not develop the social skills necessary for acceptance by peers or the larger community.

What Is the Effect of Family Identity Formation on Your Family?

Many of us expect our newly arrived child to feel like he is part of the family within weeks or months of placement. When this does not happen, we may seek out a specialist in attachment therapy to address the issue. While some of the children who hold back are experiencing reactive attachment disorder, many are not. They simply need more time, possibly years, to integrate into the family group. A child who is misdiagnosed as having attachment disorder simply because he is not bonding with the new family is at risk of being labeled as the problem within the family. Once he has that identity, it is highly probable that he will live up to it. The family is then faced with years of acting out that result from what the child innately knows to be the family's unrealistic expectations. In these situations, it is unlikely that the child will ever feel that he is a positive part of the family identity.

You may even find that you pull back emotionally from the child who is unwilling, or unable, emotionally to engage with the group. When this happens, you may begin to focus on the differences between the child and the family, rather than the similarities that could potentially bring you all together. It is understandable that you might have difficulty holding on to someone who is pushing you away, but when you pull back, your family is at high risk for disruption. And when you pull back from your child, you may find that you are pulling back from your spouse as well; and the marriage can destabilize.

Life Lesson: Family Identity Formation

Previously, Vic and Lorna had each been married, and their children from each of these marriages had grown up and were now independent. Vic and Lorna were only in their early forties though, and thought that they would like to raise a family together. After all, neither had ever really been happy in their first marriages. They both only stayed as long as they had so that their children could have a sense of stability and security. Yet, as they looked back on their decisions, they were convinced that it had not been in their children's best interest to grow up in such hostile and unhappy homes. Now that they had finally found each other, they longed to experience the normal family life they had denied themselves and their first set of children.

They thought long and hard about how to create this new family. Lorna was not really excited about the thought of going through morning sickness in her forties, and she was worried about the risk of having a child with some kind of genetic problem due to her own age. Vic, equally excited about having a new family, was not eager to start with a baby, no matter how they acquired one, as he did not want to be playing kid's soccer when he was sixty-five. So, after much deliberation and exploration of alternatives, they decided to adopt an older sibling group.

Vic and Lorna joined adoption support groups, took older-child adoption training, and scoured the Net looking at faces of sibling groups who needed a family. They were aware of the risks of attachment disorder, post-traumatic stress disorder, fetal alcohol syndrome, and all the other conditions that sent tremors of fear down their spines. However, they were convinced that if they were patient and were careful about scrutinizing the backgrounds of children proposed to them, then they would be able to avoid the most destructive characteristics, and would be able to adopt children whose needs they could meet.

It happened. After two years, and several rounds saying "no," they finally accepted a sibling group of three children. A boy, age eight, and two girls, ages seven and five. The backgrounds of the children were not too bad. They had originally been removed from their mother's care because she was drug-addicted and neglectful. However, there was no record of her drinking during pregnancy, and it appeared that she did not begin her heavy drug use until after all three were born. In fact, the older two children had good memories of her and it seemed that she had never abused them. The children each had a different father, and nothing was known of any of these men. When they were removed from the mother's care, they were placed in a foster home that had kept them until they recently became freed for adoption. They were bright children, capable of attachment, fun to be with, and eager for a family of their own; everything that Vic and Lorna had hoped for. The children would benefit from the love and security they were offering, and Vic and Lorna would finally be able to give these children what they had not been able to give their birth children. That is, parents who love each other, who could provide a warm family environment.

The settling-in period went well. The children seemed to like having parents of their own, and Vic was pleased to see that Sharda, the middle girl, shared his interest in all things musical. Lorna found that she developed an instant bond with Michael, something that surprised her as she had only raised daughters before, and had not considered that she could get so quickly attached to a boy. Their grown children often came by to visit, and were soon volunteering to baby-sit their newly adopted siblings.

The first year went by very smoothly. There were some bumps and lumps along the way. But Vic and Lorna knew that they had lucked out. They had the best children in the world. By the second year, it almost seemed as if they had always had the children, right from birth. And, by the third year, they sometimes forgot that the children were in the family by adoption. It seemed as if the children must have been born to them.

It was not until the children reached adolescence that things began to fall apart. Michael was doing well, and so was Sharda. Both were involved in sports at school, had friends from good families, and were keeping up with their academic work. It was Tiffany, the youngest, who was presenting problems. She was angry, defiant, and rebellious. Recently, she had come home with her bottom lip pierced. Vic hit the roof.

"What is it with you," he yelled at her while she was putting the antiseptic cream on the newly made wound that circled the lip ring. "Why do you have to mutilate yourself and embarrass your family?"

"This isn't mutilation, it's fashion. And you have no reason to be embarrassed by me. How I look is none of your business," Tiffany yelled back. Her lip was hurting badly and she wasn't too sure she really liked how it looked. Of course, all of her friends had warned her that she wouldn't really know what it looked like until the swelling from the piercing went down.

Lorna pushed past Vic and turned Tiffany toward her so she could see the lip.

"Did you have this done professionally, or did a friend do it?" she asked.

"What the heck does that matter?" Vic bristled. "It's ugly no matter who did it. She looks like a street kid."

"It matters because she's more at risk of infection if it wasn't done professionally. I want our doctor to see it," Lorna answered. She turned back to Tiffany. "Who did this, honey? I need to know if we need to get some ointment or something."

Tiffany was glaring at Vic through her tears. The lip hurt badly, but she was not about to let him know that. She didn't really like it, swelling or not, but she wasn't about to let him know that either.

"Melanie did it. But we used disinfectant. She did her own lip last week and some other kids at school, too. She knows what she's doing."

"Melanie did it?" Vic said, incredulous. "Melanie who? Not that foster kid who's staying with the Jacobs. She's the one whose influencing you to look like this? Why are you hanging around with her?"

"Vic," Lorna interjected. "How could you?"

"How could I what?" Vic asked.

"I'm a foster kid," Tiffany yelled, her tone matching that of Vic's only moments earlier. "Remember, I'm a foster kid and I was born to a street kid. That's my destiny."

Vic's face was ashen. "Oh honey, I'm sorry. I didn't mean what I said. It's just that you're my little girl, and I can't stand to see you do things to hurt yourself."

"Your father really didn't mean that, Tiffy," Lorna said softly. "There's nothing wrong with being a foster child, and you aren't a foster kid anyway. You are our child, you're part of our family. This is your life, your place. It's where you belong."

"No, it isn't," Tiffany replied. "I've never belonged here. I don't even want to belong here. This is just a place where I live. I don't remember my mother, I don't remember the foster parents very much, but I do remember that I didn't start here and I don't belong here. This isn't even a real family. Kathy's family is a real family. They all look like each other, and there are pictures in their house of when the kids were babies. They all know where they were born, and when they started walking and talking. We don't know any of that stuff about each other. We don't look like each other. None of us is really related to each other. We're just a bunch of rejects that somebody threw together. This isn't a family and I don't belong here!"

Challenges in Forming a Family Identity

Allow time. Do not rush the formation of family identity. It takes months and years for the changes in each individual, and in the family, to become established. The family will exist for more time after the children have grown up than it will while they are still in the home. The identity of the family can continue to form throughout the years.

Recognize that the existing family identity must transform with the addition of a new child. The identity of your family must change and be re-defined to include your new child. This means that his needs, experiences, race/ethnicity, challenges, and charms merge with those of your family to create something new. You must recognize that each time a child is added, the identity of your family as a whole must shift, change, and ultimately merge into an entity that reflects what the child has brought.

Develop family rituals. Rituals that define your family will help the child learn who this family is. Simple things, such as designating every Friday as pizza and movie night, can be helpful. It is important that the whole family help in choosing the movies. If there are different age groups to consider, you can take everyone to the video store right after school and let them each choose one video. Attending a religious service is helpful, as it provides routine as well as ritual. If organized religion is not a part of your family's life, then substitute the social and communal activities that churches provide by joining some other group, such as an environmental organization. The important thing is to say, "This is what our family does on Fridays," or "Our family always goes to church together on Sundays," or "Our family is really into race cars. We like to go to races." The rituals must not only be carried out, they must also be articulated and explained.

Do "feet." This is explained in chapter 2. You will find that it is helpful in demonstrating to your child the boundaries of the immediate family unit. "Feet" should only include those who are currently members of the household, and considered to be related. The time that the child is being massaged gives him an opportunity to feel that he is the center of his new family.

Teach the values of the family. An older child will have experienced the values of different people in a variety of different living situations, so it's important to articulate the values of this family. Do not assume that she will learn or understand this, by osmosis or by observation.

Take lots of pictures. Take pictures of the whole family, various family members, pets, etc. Be sure that the child is in each picture. Your child will enjoy looking at photographs of himself helping with cooking, walking the dog, playing with a sibling, cuddling with a parent, eating a meal with grandma, etc. These pictures present a clear, distinct symbol of the child's place in the family. Always have some new or favorite pictures on the refrigerator door. Keep the pictures in a place where the child can get to them easily. Let her pick out a few from every roll to have for herself, or to put in her own album. Do this for at least three years.

Water and candle rituals. The water ritual is done by having each person in your family represented by a small symbolic container of water. Individuals pour a small container into a larger one. When it is filled, the larger container represents the new family. It is worthwhile to spend some money on attractive and unique containers for this ritual.

In the candle ritual, every member of the family lights a candle, then places it in a container of sand. When the candles are all lit and placed, the entire family can blow out the candles together, or let them burn down. Again, it is worth spending some money on attractive, unique candles and a sand dish.

Find and define a role for your child. Your child needs to feel that she has a particular role in the family identity. Find some label that is positive and realistic. For example, one child might be very tidy and so can be called the *family tidier.* Another may know how to play the flute at school, and might be called the *family musician.* See what your child responds to. The identified role can change with time and interests. Be sure not to use a role that is more suitable to another sibling.

Create a family calendar. Let your child be in charge of a large calendar that shows important family events. A large calendar, kept in full view, will help your child recall what has happened in the family recently, and what is expected to happen, such as a family vacation or Grandpa's birthday. This creates a visual symbol of the events in the life of the family.

Do lots of things as a family. Whenever possible, choose to do things together. When you are trying to get one child to a therapist, another to gymnastics, and keep the home running it can be difficult to find the time to go bowling, to go to family-swim time, or to take family walks and picnics. However, the older child may never have had an opportunity to be part of a family that plays together, and she may not even understand that families do such things. One of your tasks in creating a family identity is to help her to understand that your family identity includes fun, as well as chores and appointments.

Have family meetings. Choose one evening a month, when the whole family sits down together, to have a general discussion about what things are important to each of you. This can be a time when allowances and curfews are renegotiated, or when summer vacation plans are discussed. It also presents a time for children to learn to have a reasonable discussion in an orderly manner. Each time, have one person act as the minutes taker, so that a record can be kept, to prevent later conflict if people don't recall what was agreed on. Begin by letting each person say what they want to bring up for discussion, and use this as an agenda. Use a "talking stick"; that is, something that a person must be holding in order to speak. It can be passed from person to person as each takes a turn. Not all issues are appropriate for this format. If you are in severe conflict with a teen over drug and school issues, those should be kept for private discussion. But, if it is a new school year, and everyone's bedtimes are going to change, this is the perfect place to decide what the time change will be.

Children can also use this format as a place to state things that they feel need to be done differently in the family, or to state how they would like to be treated in certain situations. For example, one child might state that she has been doing extra chores and that no one has noticed or appreciated her efforts; but this is not a place for children or adults to complain about each other. Anything that sounds like tattling should be avoided and saved for another time.

CHAPTER 8

Cross-Cultural and Transracial Adoption

Cross-cultural and transracial adoptions often have blurred boundaries. A transracial adoption generally refers to families in which the parents adopt a child who is of a different race. Cross-cultural adoption generally refers to situations in which the parents adopt a child from a different culture and the child may, or may not, be of the same race or ethnic background. For example, adoption of an African-American child by Caucasian parents is transracial. It may also be cross-cultural if the parents are white Americans and the child is black and from Ethiopia. Many people would also consider an African-American child placed with white parents to be a cross-cultural adoption because there are differing life experiences for people of color than for Caucasians in North America. Adoption of a white child from Russia is considered a cross-cultural adoption if the Caucasian parents are American or Canadian.

The similarities in the two types of adoption, cross-cultural and transracial, relate to the challenges presented in helping your child to proudly retain her racial or cultural identity while solidifying her identity in your family. In most adoption cases, the child is from some kind of minority group, or is a minority in her new community, and you are from the majority. Most adoptive parents are also from a higher economic bracket than that of the family from which the older child has been adopted. This means that the part of culture that is formed by economic and educational status makes most older child adoptions cross-cultural, regardless of race or country of origin.

Adoption Controversy

You have likely already learned that the topics of cross-cultural and transracial adoption are controversial. Some people believe that taking a child from his native country or racial group is an act of cultural genocide and cultural imperialism. Others feel that the child is robbed of an essential part of his birthright and identity when he is raised apart from his racial and cultural roots. Still others believe that rather than taking children from parents too poor or too disadvantaged to be able to keep their children, the money and energy currently spent on adoption would be better used to enable the birth family to stay together. Some believe that the increasing numbers of African-American children placed with Caucasian parents is a symbol of the overall oppression that has historically caused tension between the two racial groups in North America.

On the other hand, it can be argued that leaving a child in foster care, or in a poverty-ridden or war-torn nation, is also a form of cultural genocide and that adoption at least allows the child an opportunity to grow up with love, safety, and an education. Many believe that as long as the child is presented with opportunities to build cultural ties to his original heritage, he will find pride in his multiracial or multicultural identity; and that the overall culture is made stronger by the grown adoptee's survival, as well as the contributions he goes on to make to society.

For many adoptive parents, the pros and cons of these types of adoptions are drowned in the overwhelming need to parent. And the prospective adopters almost always believe that they can, and will, preserve the child's cultural or racial heritage regardless of the obstacles presented.

The Impact on Your Family Life

The impact of this type of adoption can change as your child grows older. In the toddler and primary school years, there is often great acceptance of your family, no matter how different you look from the other families in the neighborhood or at the local school. During these early years, your child may easily find a place in the community of children and children's activities. However, as he reaches the teen years, the search for identity that is common among all youth may result in his being ostracized, subjected to racial or cultural slurs, or developing feelings of lower self-esteem. Your teen might be reluctant to discuss this with you and may present a facade that all is well.

Part of your child's resistance to confronting the issue might come from shock and grief, as his longtime friends abandon him once they hit high school. Another factor might be his quick acceptance of the notion that to be different means to be inferior. This can result in depression, drug abuse, suicidal ideation, generalized anger, and rebellion. Each of these can easily begin to break down the parent/child relationship, especially when you are unaware that it is your child's difficulties with the transracial/cultural aspect of the family that is at the root of the problem.

Challenging Your Values

Adopting a child from another race or culture can also challenge your own value system as you discover that some of your friends make negative comments based on lack of information or negative stereotypes. For example, some members of your social circle may be very positive and supportive of the adoption while the child is a toddler, but then find excuses not to hire your teenaged black son for an after-school job in their small business. You might find that some of your friends make comments indicating that they have low expectations for the child's academic potential just because the child is from a Third World nation, or conversely, they may have high expectations for a child who is of Asian descent.

Prospective adoptive parents may not realize that once they adopt a child who is somehow different from them, they too will become different in the eyes of the community. The adjustment to being different, or to becoming part of a minority, can be devastating for people who have been part of the mainstream. And it may be difficult to find any place where the family is part of a larger culture. The culture of the child may reject the family for *stealing* the child, and the dominant culture may reject the family for raising the child. Emma Anne's story illustrates some of the difficulties families face in dealing with cross-cultural adoption.

Life Lesson: Transracial Adoption

Emma Anne did not really understand that she was a different race from her parents until she was fourteen. Up until then, she had understood that she was born in China, and that her parents were born here. She knew that she had black hair, and her parents' hair was brown, and she knew that her skin was a slightly different shade. She also knew that it was because she was adopted that she and her parents went to picnics with other families who had daughters who were born in China. That was why there were pictures of China and books about the country all over the house. But none of this had any personal meaning to Emma Anne until she was in ninth grade.

She had been staring at her face in the mirror for what seemed like hours. She had been combing her hair, trying to get it to go fluffy, like her mom's.

"What are you doing?" her mom asked.

"My hair. It just hangs there. No matter what I do, it won't curl or stay curled."

"Well, of course not. If you want it curled, we'll have to perm it. Chinese hair just doesn't do that on its own."

And that was when it had hit her. Chinese hair. She had Chinese hair. For the first time in her life, Emma Anne really looked at herself. Her mother's image was also reflected back at her and she could see all the differences she had never really noticed before.

"I have Chinese hair, Mom. Chinese hair," she repeated.

"I shouldn't have said it like that," her mom replied. "Asian people have beautiful hair. Look," she took the brush from Emma Anne's hand and started to brush the shoulder length hair. "It's shiny and strong and thick. And the darkness matches your eyes."

Emma Anne stared harder in the mirror. "I have Chinese eyes, too, don't I, Mom." Her chin began to quiver.

"Emma Anne, what's wrong?" her mother asked. "You know you're from China. You have friends from there, too. What is it, honey?"

"I'm never going to be like you, am I, Mom?" Emma Anne could barely get the words out. She felt like she was suffocating. Yes, she knew she was Chinese, she knew she looked different from her family, but she had never felt different. Suddenly, the differences were big, and they were gnawing out a place deep inside of her and creating a hollowness that she had not felt before.

"I don't speak Chinese, I don't remember China. But I am Chinese. How can that be, Mom?"

"Honey, why are you so upset? I don't understand. There are millions of people with Chinese heritage who are born in other countries and they don't speak Chinese and have never been there either. Anyway, there's nothing wrong with being Chinese. We've told you about how the Chinese invented all kinds of things while Westerners were barely crawling out of the caves. And we've taken you to exhibitions of Chinese art. The Chinese have a magnificent, ancient culture. You should be proud of your heritage."

"But how can it be my heritage, Mom?" Emma Anne asked. "I don't live there. I live here. I speak English. I dress American. All of my friends are from here." A look of horror crossed Emma Anne's face. "Oh Mom, who will I marry? If I marry a white boy or a black boy, my baby will be a half-breed!"

"Emma Anne, don't use that racist term. There is no such thing as a half-breed. People just are what they are. Some are one race, some are another, and some are mixed. There is nothing wrong with being any of those."

"Well, who am I supposed to marry, Mom? I don't want a mixed race baby. I want one that looks like me. But I don't know any Chinese boys. All of the other adopted Chinese kids are girls. And what if all the Chinese boys I meet are awful? I'll have to marry one anyway, just to have a Chinese baby."

Emma Anne's mother took a deep breath and then let it out slowly. "Emma Anne," she said, "you are my baby, and you don't look like me. But you know that your dad and I love you more than anything. And you can't marry anyone yet, but when you start to date, you can date whomever you choose, as long as he treats you well and can get your dad to let you out of the house." Her mom smiled.

Emma Anne looked back into the mirror. She looked at the Chinese face staring at her and tried to reconcile the image with the way she felt inside. It didn't work. She looked again at her mother's image. She knew her mother would never understand. How could she? Her mother looked just like everyone else in the family, and like most of the people in the town. Emma Anne felt very alone.

Meeting the Challenges of Cross-Cultural and Transracial Adoption

Seek out and attend courses or seminars that actively help you unlearn prejudice. Many of us do not believe we have racial or cultural prejudices, simply because we have not been challenged or confronted by them. The fact that one believes in racial and cultural equality for all does not necessarily mean that one is free from subtle prejudices that can harm the child. Contact whatever local group deals with prejudice to find out where courses or seminars are being held. If one is not available in the adoptive parents' community, the prospective parents should organize it.

Stare back. Transracial families are often stared at by strangers when in public places. People will also feel free to make comments on the mixed race of your family. In either case, be prepared to respond quickly and simply. A return stare can speak volumes about your family's right to be in the community. If the person is making comments such as, "Are those your children or are they adopted?" you can answer in any way you choose, but find a way that the family has already agreed on. Some families will prefer "That's none of your business," others will prefer "They are mine and they are adopted," others will prefer "Why do you ask?" The response is not important, only that it has been agreed upon with your child.

Consider your community. Is it a racially and culturally mixed neighborhood in which the child will be accepted as a teen as well as a toddler or child? Is it a community in which there are a variety of different families so that your transracial family does not appear unusual? Is it a community in which there is access to other transracial and cross-culture families? For the developing child, communities that have these attributes would be easier than those in which she would be the only "different" child in the area.

Consider the school. Does your local school, or the private school your family has always attended, have a variety of races and cultures represented in the classrooms, by both students and teachers? If not, enroll the child in one that does. It would be best if there are other children from her own culture or racial heritage there. If not, a school that at least has some visible diversity will mean that she does not stand out or become isolated simply because she was not born in the majority culture.

Adopt more than one child from the same culture. There are many reasons to adopt; one of the worst is to give your child a sibling. However, when making long-term, transracial or cross-cultural adoption plans, consider whether it is possible for you to adopt two or more children from the same race or culture. This will reduce her isolation and give her an ally at school. However, this should only be done if you always wanted more than one child.

Never tolerate racial or cultural slurs or jokes. Your child needs to know that any type of prejudice is wrong, and that you will never tolerate this form of humor or slur. It can be difficult if the person saying the slur is someone you love, such as a great-grandmother who is simply out of touch with the current correct words. However, your child has to know that no one is allowed to say anything bad about her race or her culture, no matter what the person's intent, no matter how important that person is to you and the family.

Seek groups, mentors, organizations, and activities from your child's race or culture. Find and develop relationships with people who are from the same background as the child. The fact that the child is Chinese or black does not mean that any Chinese person or black organization will suffice. Find those who are from the same part of China, or from the same linguistic group. A child from Ethiopia needs to be with others from Ethiopia, not just others from Africa. A child who has spent years in an inner-city foster home would do well to be linked with a successful adult who grew up in inner-city foster homes.

You should participate in the cultural activities to the extent that the child is comfortable. A young child may want you to be present and active in everything she does, and it's important for the child to witness you investing in her culture. However, as she reaches her teens, she may need for you to back off and let her be alone with her heritage as there may come a point in her development when she is embarrassed by her transracial family. She will grow out of this stage, but it needs to respected while she is in it.

Do not assume that your experience of the transracial or cross-cultural adoption is the same as your child's. You may feel that the adoption is a success because you love the child, the child has appeared to do well in life, and your family has never faced significant issues related to the racial or cultural challenge. However, your child may have always experienced a sense of loss and alienation from his own culture, but he did not feel that he had the right to express this. Also, he may have been subjected to taunts or more subtle forms of racism that he has never mentioned. Concealing this truth is done generally either to protect you or because the child feels shame and humiliation and is internalizing the prejudice.

Remember that it is harder for adolescents than for younger children. You can easily assume that all is well because no racial or cultural issues came to the fore during early childhood. However, the teen years are often a mine field of racially and culturally motivated prejudice. Friends that the child related to when younger may now be uncomfortable with the youth's request for a date. Or the white best friend may no longer be willing to go out at night with the black adoptee because he is afraid the police will hassle them. This kind of prejudice is rarely articulated by the teen adoptee, but such racism can be a significant factor in the life of an adolescent adoptee in a transracial family.

Seek out other adoptive families of mixed race or culture. You have more in common with the subculture of adoption than with either of the races or cultures involved. You and your child need the reinforcement that comes from spending time with other transracial or cross-cultural families who were created through adoption and who face the same challenges. If such a group does not exist in the community, start one.

Seek out culture camps. There are several culture camps advertised in national adoption magazines. These provide you and your child with the chance to experience being the majority culture for an intense period of time. It also gives the child or youth an opportunity to spend quality time with other children of the same heritage who can share the joys and the pains of growing up in an adoptive transracial family.

Develop ongoing personal relationships with members of the child's heritage. It is not enough to attend special ceremonies or holiday events. That is the equivalent of cultural tourism. Your child needs ongoing relationships with other members of his heritage, and you need these people to teach you about what the child is experiencing as she grows. Mentors and friends can teach your child how to deal with the racism and can teach you how to spot the more subtle forms.

Find doctors, dentists, piano teachers, etc., that are from the same cultural group or racial heritage as your child. Your child needs to see that people who look or sound like her have an important, and routine, place in her life and in the community. She also needs to see that you seek them out as authorities on important matters, such as health, and that you rely on their skills and abilities.

Find hairdressers who are of the same racial or ethnic origins as your child. Hair care differs for different races. People who come from the same origins as your child will have experience and knowledge about hair care that you do not have. Also, the child may like being touched by people who look or sound like her. This kind of informal, casual touch can be a symbolic connection to her own origins that you cannot provide.

Educate your child about racism and intolerance. Help her to understand that it is the person who is saying those things that has the problem, not her. Also, help her to understand that intolerance takes many forms and is rooted in ignorance and hatred.

Look for racism and intolerance. If you are a member of the cultural and racial majority in your community, then you may not even realize when some acts or words are based in racism and intolerance. For example, when there are groups of children waiting to be served at a candy stand, is your child the last to be waited on? This may or may not be racism, but you need to be watching for it because your child will notice it even if you don't. She will need your support and help when these types of encounters occur.

CHAPTER 9

Temporary Care

Even when all the information is available and the supports are in place, there may still come a time when you cannot cope with the behaviors your child is presenting. This can happen when you have reached your limits of exhaustion and tolerance and the rest of the family is nearly breaking up due to the behaviors of the child. You and your child may be well bonded, but the child may still present behaviors that are beyond the coping ability and skills of your family.

It is not uncommon for adoptive families to find that when they reach out to social services for help, they are blamed; the child is seen as the victim of demanding and unreasonable adoptive parents. This kind of attitude can widen the gulf between you and your child instead of narrowing it. The legislation in some states and some provinces can serve to create a permanent dissolution. Many jurisdictions do not allow the time that is required for you and your child to resolve the issues, before returning custody to the state.

In most situations, placing a child back into foster care does not have to result in a permanent dissolution of the adoption. The time in foster care can be used to help the rest of the family members recoup their emotional strength, and to determine if they can resume living together. Even for those families who cannot return to living together, the relationship between parents and child, and between siblings and child, does not have to be severed. In all but a few cases, the parents and child can continue to have a relationship that is based on love and respect even if it does not include living together. The child's ties to her adoptive family deserves the same respect as her ties to her family of origin. Neither the child nor the adoptive family benefit from a needless, permanent separation.

Impact of Temporary Care on Your Family

If you reach a point where you are unable to cope with your child's behaviors, you may find that you are blamed by everyone, including yourself. Guilt, depression, and internalized anger can develop. As a result, your marital relationship can suffer. Other children in your family may have been neglected while the acting-out child sucked up all of your attention; so, they may be experiencing depression and require therapy to help them sort through their feelings.

It is likely that the problems have been going on for some time before the decision to remove the child is made. Your home may have become a war zone and the ongoing hostilities can result in exhaustion or in stress-induced physical symptoms, such as headaches, lowered resistance to viruses, and changes in sleeping and eating patterns. Not only can marital problems arise, but you may find that you or your spouse have developed stress-related problems that can impair your health and affect your workplace performance. This is the situation Jay and Evelyn found themselves in.

Life Lesson: When Things Go Too Far

Jay and Evelyn adopted Neal when he was five years old. He had been in foster care most of his young life, living mainly with one family for the three years prior to adoption. They knew that Neal had been prenatally exposed to drugs and alcohol; but he was developing on schedule, he did not seem to have any attachment issues, and he was full of joy and cuddles. Jay bonded with Neal very quickly, and Evelyn soon after. The first few years were filled with soccer games, swimming lessons, and buddies. Neal had some learning disabilities, but Evelyn and Jay enrolled him in a supplemental learning program and he was able to keep up academically with his peers. All in all, it seemed like an ideal adoption. It was so good, in fact, that Jay and Evelyn adopted two more children. For a few years, they felt like they had the family they had always dreamed of.

Then Neal entered adolescence. Almost overnight, the cheerful and happy boy they had been raising turned into a brooding and surly youth who wanted nothing from his parents except an increase in his allowance and total freedom. Neal began skipping his learning program classes, and then outright refusing to go. He also began skipping school and he dropped his old friends to hang out with a crowd of kids who smoked, drank, and were sexually active. When Evelyn confronted Neal on the issue of quitting the learning program, Neal was outraged.

"They make me look dumb," he yelled at Evelyn. "I'm not a dummy and I don't need them."

"I know you aren't a dummy, Neal, but you do need them to keep up your grades," Evelyn replied. "You want to go to college, don't you?"

"Maybe I don't," Neal said, still yelling. "I don't need school to be a band roadie."

"A band roadie?" asked Evelyn.

"Yeah, those are the guys who travel with the big bands and handle all their equipment. It's so cool. Hanging out with famous musicians. Girls and dope all over the place. It's cool."

Evelyn let the conversation drop. She knew better than to argue with someone who aspired to be a band roadie. The couple once again sought the help of the therapist who had helped them with Neal in the early days of the adoption.

"What happened to him?" Jay asked. "Did we do something wrong? Have we missed something? He used to be so wonderful, but now he's nothing but a jerk. He's rude to us, he stays out half the night, and I found marijuana in his room last week. What happened?"

"The first five years of his life happened," the therapist answered. "He has anger he's never dealt with, grief and loss he's never confronted, and he's expressing it the only way he knows how. By acting out his anger against the world."

"We came to see you for two years. You said he was doing well," Evelyn reminded the therapist.

"He was doing well. But there are only so many emotional issues that a child can resolve. He needed to get on with being a little boy, so we ended therapy. Now he's finding his own way to tell the world what he feels, and to find out what he needs in return."

"That sounds just great," Evelyn said sarcastically. "We have to deal with a great kid who is throwing his life away. And we have to live with the worry. I never know if he's coming home at night. I dread every day that I'll get a telephone call from the police saying they have him in jail, or worse, that he's dead of a drug overdose. I want to know what to do for my son," Evelyn demanded.

"All you can do for your son right now is to hang in there. If he will come for counseling, we can work on some of the issues, but there isn't going to be an overnight return of the sweet boy you have loved all these years."

For the next two years, Jay and Evelyn followed the therapist's advice and hung in there. They hung in there when Neal would not come home for days at a time. They hung in there when he stole from their wallets. They hung in there when he got suspended from school and then expelled. They hung in there when he swore at them. They hung in there when he came home drunk or stoned.

When he was fifteen, they could no longer hang in there. Neal was jailed for the second time, for theft. He had stolen a car. Since he did not know how to drive, he had turned a corner too fast and the car had spun out of control, hitting another car and injuring the driver. When the police arrived on the scene, they found Neal under the influence of alcohol. The police kept Neal in juvenile jail for a week, then released him to his parents. The court case was set for later in the year. That night, Neal gave L.S.D. to his ten-year-old brother. When Jay walked in on them both high, he knew he had finally reached his limit. The next morning, he called social services and asked them to remove Neal from the family home. He and Evelyn were no longer willing to have Neal around the younger children, nor were they able to keep worrying about him or fighting with him on a daily basis. They were filled with a jumble of conflicting feelings. They were exhausted, overwrought, hurt, and angry. Although they knew it was not reasonable, they could not help but feel betrayed by the son they so loved.

Managing a Temporary Care Arrangement

No parent is eager to place his or her child into temporary care, but there are ways to maintain contact with your child and save your relationship from flickering out.

Maintain the relationship. Do not be bullied by social services. You have the right and the responsibility to maintain a relationship with your child, even though social workers or counselors may be creating obstacles to the relationship. Go to the supervisors, government officials, or outside sources of advocacy to ensure that the relationship is preserved. This means that you maintain the right to visit your child, to have your child visit the family home on certain occasions, to participate in your child's life by watching him at sports or school events, to continue sharing in educational decisions and receive a copy of the report card, to have regular telephone contact, and to ensure that the child is placed in an alternate living situation with caregivers who will work with, not against, you.

Remember that adoption is a lifelong commitment. Even though someone else may have to finish raising your child, you can still have a relationship with him as an adult. That means being a grandparent to his children, sharing time together at Christmas or holidays, and staying in touch through calls and visits.

Continue to tell the child that he has a place in your family. Be clear with your child that he is still a member of your family even though he has to be in foster care or a residential treatment setting. Help him to understand that his last name will not change and that he still belongs in your family.

Use extended family members to bridge the hostility gap. If either you or the child are still too angry to have a peaceful meeting during the first few weeks or months after she goes into foster care, then ask older siblings, grandparents, or an aunt or uncle to do the visiting until tempers have cooled down. This will allow her to understand that she is still a valued part of the family, but will not create yet another scenario for confrontation. However, make sure that it is a family member who is able and willing to be neutral and loving toward her.

Do not feel guilty for what has happened, but be responsible about what will happen. In other words, don't waste time and energy feeling like a failure over events that have already happened. Take concrete action to create something positive with your child. This may mean counseling to help you get a dispassionate look at what you need to be doing for the child in the long term. Or, it may mean actively working with the social worker and foster parents on building a healthier relationship with the child.

Take some time out, refocus, and rebuild. Once your child has entered foster care or a treatment center, take time out from the stress. Refocus the family energy. Stop talking about the things that went wrong, or the negative behaviors. A therapist can help everyone debrief, but outside of counseling sessions, find other things to talk about. Usually, during the months or years before the child leaves the home, the acting-out child has been the focal point of the family's attention and discussions. This is the time to start finding other people and things on which to put energy and time.

At first, you may just want to sleep and rest. Siblings may also need to sleep and recoup the energy that the conflict has taken from them. After a few days or weeks of this, start filling in the energy void with healthy activities. Join a group that has nothing to do with children, get active in the garden, or put more time into the neglected workplace.

This is also a time to rebuild the relationships that have suffered while the child was acting out. Other children in the home may have felt neglected as your attention all went to the one child. The siblings will be feeling abused by the acting-out child, and will need special attention and time from you in order to heal from their experiences of recent months. Extended family and friends may have felt alienated as you developed a siege mentality while dealing with the everyday conflicts and hostilities. Take this opportunity to spend time with them. Work to get back on track with friends and loved ones.

Remember that the negative feelings will pass. The feelings of anger, despair, hopelessness, loss, and betrayal will pass with time. These are common feelings during a crisis, but they will fade as the mental exhaustion reduces.

Do not take your child back into the home before your family is ready. Crowded caseloads will result in most social workers trying to return the child to the home as soon as possible. However, if he returns before all family members have healed and are ready to deal with him again, such a plan is doomed to fail. Resist efforts for a premature return and, again, use outside advocates if necessary. The most common threat by social workers is that if the child does not return soon, you will lose custody. That is a risk that must be faced. However, loss of custody does not mean loss of relationship. Contact can continue and you can readopt the child at a later date.

Document everything. From the point at which the plan is developed to have your child leave the home, you should begin documenting every contact with the child, the social worker, the foster parents, the therapists, and others involved. Let everyone know you're keeping a record. It's a good idea to write down minutes of each meeting and send them back to each participant. This can prevent confusion later about what the plans for reconciliation are and what each party has agreed to do at every phase of the temporary out-of-home care.

Know the legislation. Have a lawyer explain all of the legislation regarding custody and the services provided. Some parents have thought they were placing their child in foster care for a specific length of time, only to find later they couldn't get him returned. Or, they thought they would have full access, only to be told that they couldn't see their child at all.

CHAPTER 10

Open Adoption

The term *open adoption* refers to an adoption in which the adoptee and the adoptive family remain in contact with at least one member of the child's birth family. The term covers many forms of contact. It can be fully confidential with the adoptive family sending a picture of the child to the birth parents through the agency, or it can be fully open, so that the birth parents have almost unrestricted access to the child.

In the case of older-child adoption, this can become a complicated situation. The child may have had a recent relationship with the birth parents or the location of the birth parents may have been lost years ago, as the child traveled through the foster care system. In other situations, one parent or both parents may be deceased or their whereabouts unknown. In some instances, the court may order that there be no parental contact with the child, in order to protect the child from dangerous birth parents, yet the child can pick up the phone and call them whenever she wishes, thereby circumventing the intent of the court to protect the child.

Factors to Consider

When you adopt an older child, it can be a significant challenge to find a balance between the needs of the child, the needs of the birth parent, your own needs, and what the courts and children's protective services believe are in the best interest of the child. All may have differing views of how much openness in the adoption is best. And what is best for the child, the members of the birth family, and for you may be in conflict. In these cases, the best interests of the child should take precedence; but not all parties may agree on what degree of openness is in the best interests of the child.

The older child may have had terrible experiences with his birth family, yet he still needs to have some contact with them, in order to be assured that the parent is alive, or to reassure himself that he has not been completely abandoned by them. Some children have only vague memories of their birth parents and have not seen them in years; but they still yearn for some kind of contact or, at least, for some current information. Children who have been in the parent role with their mother, father, or both may feel that the parent is at risk of dying without their care and support. The parentified child may also believe that his siblings will not survive without his care. These concerns place tremendous stress on the older adoptee and can become an obstacle to attachment with you.

You may find it difficult to accept that an abusive or negligent parent has the right to remain in contact with your child, especially if you feel that you rescued the child from a bad situation. You may also believe that the parent belongs in prison for what she or he has done to the child. The birth parent may actually be in prison either for crimes against the child or unrelated offenses. Most adoptive parents do not normally socialize with people who have the kind of problems that lead to abuse or neglect. You may have never knowingly been friends with a person with a substance abuse problem or personally known a person with a severe mental illness. This inexperience can lead you to feel overwhelmed and confused by the child's need for contact with such troubled parents.

Children have varying needs for contact with their birth parents. Some want full contact, some want restricted access, and some want to reestablish lost ties. Other children may not want any contact at all. They may have little or no memory of the birth family or they may have terrifying memories. Still others may have an attachment disorder or a behavior disorder that precludes any interest in anybody from their past or present. In some cases, children aren't aware that they have grandparents or other extended family members who cannot care for them but would like to provide support through birthday cards and the occasional phone call. Often, these relatives are not discovered until the final termination process is before the courts.

In some cases, the birth parents do not wish to have contact after the child has been placed for adoption. They may find it too painful to maintain a relationship, or they may be so ashamed of their inability to parent that they cannot continue to face the child. Severe addiction problems or mental health problems can make a birth parent's life so unmanageable that he or she can't maintain contact.

The Importance of Open Adoption

In the early 1970s, researchers began to document what adoptees had been saying for years—that for many, complete separation from their family origins was a source of severe emotional and psychological distress. A major issue is the right of the adoptee, like every other citizen, to access her own birth information. Birth parents, too, started to speak out against the permanent separation from children they could not raise. Many began to demand at least some form of ongoing contact with children placed for adoption. Many adoptive parents also fought for their children's right to have information about, and contact with, members of their family of origin.

From that point forward, secrecy in adoption has been under open attack and has resulted in significant changes in adoption laws and in adoption practices. For example, many jurisdictions now have government run reunion registries, as well as open birth records. Adoption agencies now include the topic of openness in their pre-adoption training for prospective adopters, and most offer some kind of contact between birth parents and infants after placement.

The Impact of Openness on Your Family

You may be challenged by the concept of openness in any form. You may have been well prepared to deal with the effect of your child's behaviors, but not with the effect of the negative behaviors or dysfunctional lifestyle of the birth family. Some adoptive parents even feel that they are unable to "claim" the older child as their own if they have to openly acknowledge, and deal with, the birth family. It can be difficult to hear your child refer to another person as "Mom" or "Dad." Many adoptive parents mistakenly feel that they must be the only parents in their child's life in order to function as a family unit. Children in the adoptive family may also find it difficult to listen to their new sibling talk about other siblings or other grandparents and parents. There may even be jealousy between unrelated siblings, if one child receives presents from relatives and another does not.

Your family may resent the intrusion of the birth family in their lives and may resist including a grandparent or uncle at the child's family birthday parties. Some adoptive parents may even find that they are jealous of the preexisting relationship between the child and a member of the birth family, and find excuses to exclude that person from contact or participation in significant events in the child's life.

Geography can also cause problems. You may initially agree to visits between the child and birth family, but then find that you are unable to afford the travel costs. If this leads you to forego other family events in order to finance the visits, then siblings will become resentful. How do you explain skipping the annual family vacation so that the new adoptee can see his or her birth family?

If birth parents don't consistently follow through with visitation plans, your older child may act out in anger, or direct destructive behaviors toward you. You may also find that after such visits, your child experiences intense grief or rage. Problems like these may require therapeutic intervention and support, as well as make you resistant to further contact with the birth family. Charles and Francine's story will help you to understand the complications of open adoption.

Life Lesson: Opening Up
to Extended Family

Charles and Francine were very proud of their semi-open adoption with the birth mothers of their first two children. At birth, these girls had been placed for adoption by young moms who had made the plans after counseling and careful consideration of what was best for themselves and their babies. Each year, Charles and Francine had dutifully sent Carly's mom a picture and an update of her activities. Elena's mom had visited several times in the first two years of the adoption, but then married and moved to the other coast. Now, contact had dwindled to phone calls, and presents on birthdays and special holidays. Neither of the girls' fathers had wanted to be involved, but Elena's paternal grandmother sent cards and presents. In return, Charles and Francine provided her with pictures once a year.

When Carly and Elena were ages seven and nine, Charles and Francine decided to adopt again. They decided that since they were now experienced parents, they could handle the complications that would come with parenting an older child. Francine also liked the idea because she didn't want to take much time off work. She had recently returned to her interrupted career, and while she was pleased to take a few months off for the first stages of adjustment, she was even more pleased that she would need only a leave of absence, and wouldn't be starting over at the bottom of her career ladder. After much thought and many conversations, Charles and Francine decided to apply for another girl, age five or six.

Charles and Francine, as well as Carly and Elena, were delighted when the social worker called to propose a five-year-old child named Ava. They rushed through the visits and the paperwork and were nearing the time of placement when the social worker brought up the issue of openness. The birth mother, an active drug addict, was not requesting any form of contact, but the father was. He was currently in prison on drug-related charges and would not be released for three years. However, he had made it clear that he wanted letters and phone calls while he remained incarcerated. Also, he wanted visits once he was released. His mother also wanted ongoing visits. When Ava was a baby, this paternal grandmother had frequently cared for her when her mother was missing and her father was in jail. Grandma had only decided not to raise her herself when her husband was diagnosed with early stage Alzheimer's. She had been to every one of Ava's school events and birthday parties and was not about to be left out of these activities in the future. More complicated still, Ava's birth father had two younger children by his second wife, and Ava had a relationship with them, as well. Ava had even lived with her stepmother and her half-siblings for two years before her father went to prison. Although the marriage had ended, Ava's birth dad wanted the half-siblings to grow up knowing each other. The social worker agreed that it would not be good for Ava to lose any more people from her life.

Charles and Francine were flabbergasted. They had considered many scenarios but none had included developing a relationship with grandparents, associating with a major criminal, or coping with half-siblings. The idea of orchestrating that much visitation and contact was daunting. The social worker, however, would not back down on the openness.

"This has to happen if you want to adopt Ava," she told them. "She has an established relationship with her grandparents, and she has always had letters and calls from her father. The father only agreed to terminate his rights when we agreed to full openness. And, since he was a decent father, it would have dragged out in court till he was released."

"But he's a criminal," Charles stated. "I don't want that kind of element in my home or near my children."

"I can understand your concern, but he isn't a violent man. His crimes have never included weapons and he has no history of domestic violence or child abuse. He even had custody of Ava till he went to prison, and he never hurt her. In fact, our records indicate that he was a pretty good dad. He never left her alone. He had her in daycare and they reported that she was always clean and well cared for. And the grandmother is an important part of her life, too. We were going to give her custody of Ava, but she withdrew when she realized she was going to have a full plate with an ill husband." The social worker sighed. "This is all a part of the package that is Ava. If you want to adopt her, then you have to accept her family as well."

"But we'll be her family," Francine exclaimed. "We have contact with our other girls' birth families, but they don't try to be parents. It sounds like these people want to be fully acknowledged as father and grandparents, and that we have to include them as part of our lives, as part of our family."

"That's right. This child will have two families. One that raises her, one that visits her, and both who love her."

"But they live all over the place," Charles interjected. "Even if we could cope with all the people, how would we arrange it all? The grandmother lives on the West Coast, and the stepmother moves to a new city every year. We'd have to pay for it all, wouldn't we? We'd use up our vacations just going from one family member to the other. We'd never have the time or money left to take the kids to Disneyland or to do any of the kind of vacationing we like to do with them. And are we supposed to give our name and address to a man who is serving time in a federal prison? I mean, he may not have been dangerous when he went into prison, but he won't have learned Miss Manners etiquette while he's there. He's a serious enough drug dealer to get federal time. You can't expect us to expose our new child and our family to that kind of man. And what if he wants her back when he gets out? This isn't a guy who is going to hire a lawyer and go to court. He could just come and kidnap her from school or take her by force from our home!"

"I know this is asking a lot, but it's what Ava needs. These people are important to her and she has a bonded relationship with each of them. If you want her, you have to take them."

Managing an Open Adoption

An open adoption can be complicated, but in most situations it can be made manageable with planning and work. The tips below can help you deal with openness in adoption.

Focus on what is best for your child. Your child is the person whose life is most affected by the separation from the birth family and by the subsequent adoption. She also has had the least influence on the decisions made about her life. Adoption is meant to improve her life and her emotional stability; therefore, her needs are the most important.

Involve a neutral third party. A therapist who is experienced in the issues of openness with older-child adoption can help determine the extent of openness that is best for the child. When negotiations between the birth family and you become difficult, it's best to involve a skilled mediator to find a measure of openness that will work for all. The social worker who handles the adoption may not be the best person to determine the child's needs or to mediate. He may have his own vested interests and may not be fully trained in issues related to openness.

Consider personal values. You may be challenged by associating with birth parents who have a different lifestyle than you do. Poverty, substance and alcohol addiction, mental illness, criminal behaviors, parental fetal alcohol syndrome, chronic unemployment, prostitution, child abuse, and domestic violence aren't generally part of the current lifestyle of the adopting family, and previously, you may not have really considered the beliefs you hold about people who live with these issues. If you scrutinize your attitudes, and if you learn to relate to the birth parents respectfully, you will be more successful in an open adoption. This can present a serious challenge to successful openness, but if it is in the child's best interests to have an ongoing relationship with the birth family, learn to do so in a manner that doesn't make the child feel ashamed of his origins.

Consider what the term "family" means to you. When you adopt an older child, it's important to consider how you perceive the concept of family in relation to the child. If you cannot accept that the older child has legitimate ties to both the family of origin and your family, then the child will have to reject either the family of origin or you. Such a choice is overwhelming and cruel for the older child, and generally results in acting-out behaviors or in the breakdown of the adoptive placement. Even when the child doesn't have ongoing ties to the birth family, she often has feelings of belonging to them or longing to be with them. This doesn't detract from her ability to commit and attach to you. It is simply a matter of feelings and needs. When you can accept your child's conflicting or ambivalent feelings about where she fits in with both families, you can support her in her confusion and ultimately strengthen the adoptive family unit.

Over time, be flexible and willing to change the agreement. The openness agreement may change or evolve over time. The birth family may want to increase or decrease involvement; the child may need more or less contact as he grows older and faces different life challenges. Birth parents who could not care for a child a few years ago may find that they can parent younger siblings. As their parenting abilities improve, they may demand increased contact with the child whom they initially chose to give up for adoption.

Use a neutral setting or a neutral supervisor for visits. If conflict between you and the birth family cannot be resolved, hire a neutral visit supervisor who can access a neutral setting for visits. This is a last resort for situations in which there have been several unsuccessful attempts to mediate a relationship between the two sets of parents.

Set reasonable safety rules. The third-party mediator can help to establish some of the rules around personal contact. For example, if the birth parent has an active substance abuse addiction, the openness agreement can include that the parent does not have contact with the child while under the influence of the substance. The agreement would have to include a plan of action to take if the parent should show up under the influence. If the parent has a history of violence toward the child or others, the agreement can specify visits occur at a neutral, safe place. However, the agreement does not have to be so detailed that it lays out rules or expectations for situations that are not likely to occur. For example, if the mother is a prostitute, the agreement does not have to state that she not bring a client on visits, or that she not discuss her form of work with the child. The likelihood of any birth parent ever doing this is very low. If the birth parent does behave in unreasonable ways, then the agreement can be modified.

Consider the power imbalance. Generally speaking, birth parents of older children are not living middle-class lifestyles at the time of placement. They are usually living below the poverty line, have minimal job skills, and have had minimal educational opportunities. The lifestyle you live may be intimidating and unfamiliar to the birth parents or to their extended family members. If they appear rude or abrupt, they may, in fact, be nervous or have different social skills and expectations.

Provide nonjudgmental support for your child's feelings. When birth parents don't live up to their part of the openness agreement, by failing to show up for visits, send cards, or telephone at birthdays as promised, your child may feel rejected or abandoned. Don't blame or shame the birth parents. The anger that you feel when your child is disappointed and let down is understandable, but it must be dealt with away from the child. Your child needs to have his hurt acknowledged and supported by you, but it won't help him if he knows that his "new" parents hate his "old" parents. It will simply create conflicted feelings and divided loyalties for the child. Acknowledge and validate your child's pain and disappointment, but refrain from making negative statements about the parents. You can let the child know that you understand that he doesn't like it when the parent fails to show up at the appointed time, but don't say that the parent doesn't seem to care, or is probably too stoned to show, or in jail. You can say that you don't like it when he is hurt like this, and that you wish the birth parents could manage their lives in a more effective manner. However, any shaming or blaming of the parents will backfire at a later date.

A therapist can help the child come to terms with the reason why the parent is unreliable. For example, she can help the child to understand that whatever problem causes the unreliability is part of the larger problem that first led to the child being placed in foster care and later adopted.

Accept the child's repeated grieving. Children may grieve after each contact whether in person or by mail or telephone call. This is normal and doesn't mean that the contact should be stopped. It also doesn't mean that the child would prefer to live with the birth family instead of you. What it means is that your child is appropriately expressing his feelings of loss and that he won't develop secondary problems from unresolved grief.

CHAPTER 11

The "Oops Response"

Most adoptive families know there will be an end to the honeymoon stage. Eventually, you and your child won't be able to present only your best behavior, and the unresolved issues and subtle adjustment challenges will begin to confound the smooth running of your family. If you first saw the child's hoarding of food as a cry for help, you may become fed up with cleaning rotting sandwiches from under the bed mattress. The child who was doing everything to please you has realized that you aren't perfect, and begins to feel angry or tricked that his new life is not like the fantasy family he longed for. He is no longer as eager to please you. This stage is normal and can be worked through, with time and support. The "oops response," however, is not the same.

Recognizing the "Oops Response"

The "oops response" may occur right at the beginning of the placement or sometime after the honeymoon phase. It's not based on adjusting from fantasy to reality, nor is it based on unresolved issues from the past. The "oops response" is when you realize that your child has personality traits that you don't like, have never liked in other people, and will never like in this child. These traits become an obstacle to your willingness to find common ground with the child.

Such traits in the child are not the result of past trauma and they are not temporary. They are inborn, normal behaviors or attitudes that will be part of the child her entire life. Exactly what it is that makes a child "unlikeable" to parents differs in each relationship. It can happen in birth families and in infant adoptions as well as in older child placements. However, when the parents have a relationship with a child from the first days of her life, they develop the attachment before they know how she will be as an older child. They have a relationship that is established well before personality is apparent. In older-child placements, you must bond to the child either because, or in spite, of your child's innate personality.

Social workers do their best to find the appropriate family for each child. They look for parents who have, in some way, demonstrated an ability to create and maintain a long-term commitment, despite challenges: parents who have the personal attributes and parenting skills necessary to meet the needs of a specific child. But no one can accurately predict whether or not there will be an emotional match between the parents and the child. Despite the many pre-placement visits, and the apparently successful early adjustment of the child and family, there can be a fundamental mismatch between the child and parents. When the parent realizes this, the response is, "Oops, what have I done?"

At this point you may consider stopping the adoption only to find there are many reasons why it is too late. Your child has become established in the school and the community, and is starting to believe that this is the family that will raise him to adulthood. Friends, family, and church members see your child as part of your family and have all responded positively to your accepting an older child. You worry that removing the child will cause irrevocable harm to his ability to trust and bond to anyone else, and will damage the emotional security of the other children in your home. Besides these concerns, there is pressure not to be viewed by the community as a failure or a cruel person. Nor do you wish to see *yourself* as a failure, or to publicly acknowledge that you do not like one of your own children. When you entered into the adoptive relationship with commitment and determination to succeed, you were well aware that a human being cannot be "returned" simply because you do not like the way he walks, talks, breathes through his mouth, lacks interest in sports or music, is less intellectual than other members of the family, or doesn't get excited about things that are important to you. While these traits seem simple and unimportant on the surface, they can be symptoms of a strong and permanent emotional mismatch between you and your child.

How the "Oops Response" Effects Your Family

When you realize you may never feel close to your adopted child, it's unlikely you will share this with anyone. The embarrassment and shame become a secret that further separates you from your child and isolates you from potential peer support. The secrecy and isolation result in the "oops" feeling becoming larger and more of an obstacle to the parent/child relationship. You may begin to see typical child misbehaviors as greater than they typically are, projecting your basic dislike of the child onto every mistake she makes. The other children in the home will sense the distance and unspoken dislike between you and the child and may begin to scapegoat her, pushing her further and further out of the family circle. Or the child may sense your dislike, and attempt to establish an alliance with your spouse, with siblings, or with someone outside of the family. Your exclusion from this relationship can create an "us versus them" feeling within the home. Max and Patty's story illustrates the "oops response" and how it affects the family.

Life Lesson: Coping with Dislike

Max and Patty were the adoptive parents of seven children who joined the family as two sets of siblings. The first, Kinesha, Rayette, and Georgia, had arrived when Kinesha was newly born, Rayette was three, and Georgia was five. The first few years had been busy and filled with therapists, support groups, and special preschools. But they had been fun years. The girls had done well, and Max and Patty often forgot that the children had even been adopted. When all the girls were in school, the couple decided to adopt again. They initially planned to request a small sibling group of younger children, but one late night, Patty was browsing through the state photo listings and found herself drawn to a sibling group of four *older* children. They were Kristin, age eight, Deshawn, age nine, Donelda, age ten, and Michael, age thirteen. Max was not as certain about adopting so many at once, and he was very uncertain about adopting such older children. But Patty found herself going back to their picture over and over again. There was something about their engaging smiles and beautiful eyes that captured her heart. Max finally relented.

Pre-placement visits went well and the children moved in just before Christmas. Max loved his girls, and found Kristin and Donelda to be very sweet. And Deshawn and Michael's high energy levels and sports interests made him realize how nice it was not to be the only man in a large family. He was soon coaching the boys' soccer team, taking them for haircuts, and browsing through the major sports marts. Michael was just beginning to get interested in girls, and Max got a real kick out of helping his new son figure out the intricacies of getting a girl's attention without looking like a fool.

The two sibling groups were merging well, too. Donelda and Rayette were the same age, but Donelda was put into a different class at school, so there was no direct competition between them. They seemed to have the same interests and the same academic skills, so they soon became best friends as well as sisters.

The final papers were signed without a problem and the family had a big dinner that was attended by several members of their extended families, and some from the neighborhood and church as well. Everyone commented on what wonderful parents Max and Patty were, and how lucky the children were to be part of such a loving family. There was a lot of hugging, a lot of thanking each other for being so wonderful.

"Okay, you were right," Max said one night after he tucked the boys in bed. "This was a good idea. We lucked out and got the best kids in the world." He grinned happily as he settled into his easy chair to read the paper. "I never thought it would work with such older kids, but this has turned out just great. No diapers, no feedings, no preschool schedules. They can walk to and from school, and we can turn our backs on them for more than five minutes. They even make their own beds once in a while, do some vacuuming, and put a dish or two in the dishwasher. We don't have to spend our entire evenings reading stories to them and bathing them either." He sighed contentedly. "I'll say it again. You were right about adopting older kids."

Patty smiled. She knew she was right. At least mostly right. The children had adjusted well. She had begun attending her adoption support group again, but that was mostly to figure out how to manage a large family, not because of any major issues. These children did not have any attachment problems, they were loving and affectionate, and despite some minor learning disabilities with Michael and Deshawn, they were all settling in well, at school and at home. There wasn't even any clear line between the two sibling groups. The seven children fought or got along depending on the issue and their moods, not on genetic ties. Kristin, Donelda, Deshawn, and Michael had received years of therapy while in foster care, and their foster parents were highly skilled people who had done a wonderful job, so even most of their more serious past traumas had been resolved to the point where they no longer interfered with their ability to function in a family.

Patty's smile tightened and disappeared. She left the room and sat alone at the kitchen table. Despite all that was so good in this adoption, she was not happy. Although the adoption was generally more success-ful than she had hoped, there was one major problem. She did not like Donelda. The feeling had not been there at the beginning. Donelda was a pretty little girl who charmed everyone. She was helpful and had a sunny personality. But, over the last year, as the honeymoon stage ended and the family began to relate in a more honest manner, Patty was finding many things about Donelda that she simply did not like. Donelda was picky. She could find something wrong in anything. She was also physically slow. Patty was compulsive about being on time, even with the seven children in tow, but they always had to wait for Donelda. She was a slob, too. Her room was a mess, her place at the table was a mess, and she looked a mess at the end of the day. So far, all of Patty's normally successful methods of teaching a child how to clean up after herself were failing. Donelda also had a spiteful side to her. It didn't lead to anything dangerous or harmful for anyone, but it was something that Patty had to watch for constantly. Patty was even finding that Donelda needed too many hugs from her. Every time she turned around, there was Donelda with her arms out, like a two-year-old wanting to be picked up. Patty knew that this need for physical reassurance was natural in an older child adoptee, but she felt herself cringe every time she had to hug the child. Furthermore, Donelda was a cheater. Whenever Donelda and Rayette played a board game, there was always some kind of conflict, resulting in Rayette finally giving up. Patty didn't like to always side with Rayette, but she couldn't help her-self. She knew that a child with a less easygoing and forgiving personal-ity than Rayette's would not have put up with Donelda's small lies and large cheats, and Patty often felt compelled to intervene when she saw what Donelda was up to, even when Rayette was not complaining.

Patty knew that Donelda had to sense some kind of coldness com-ing from her. Perhaps that was why the child tried so hard to get her attention all the time and constantly initiated those childish hugs. But Patty found that she was withdrawing further and further from this daughter. She even looked for excuses to send Donelda out of the room when the two of them were alone for more than a couple of minutes.

"What is it with me?" she wondered to herself. She knew that Donelda also had many good attributes. She was very kind to animals and to other children. She was the first to volunteer to help one of the others look for a lost toy, and she was always willing to help her siblings with their homework. Donelda did not steal, she was not violent, she did not hoard, she did not self-mutilate, she was respectful to adults at home and at school, and she was a good student. So many positives yet none of them seemed to overcome the increasing number of negatives that Patty saw every time she looked at the child. "What am I going to do about this?" she asked herself.

Patty had tried to talk to a few people about this growing problem. Max had not understood.

"What do you mean you don't think you like her much? How can you not like one of our own children? She's a sweetheart. I'm sure you are just feeling tired today," he said.

Her mother had told her that she would get over it. "You wanted all of these children, and you are the one who told me to look for the positives. Well, I've looked, and there seems to be a lot of good in that girl. Maybe you just took on more than you could handle and you are blaming it on her. Anyway, it doesn't matter. You will find a way to cope, you always do."

A couple of the women at her support group had laughed at her concerns and commented on how difficult their children were. "You're complaining because she cheats at board games? When my daughter was Donelda's age, she got herself permanently expelled from school for stalking a teacher, then sending him threatening notes and setting fire to his classroom. I had to pay a fortune to put her in a private school, where she did the same thing."

"My son was already taking drugs at Donelda's age," said the second mother. "Donelda doesn't even swear or smoke cigarettes."

Patty knew that she was not going through the same type of problems these women were talking about. This was not about managing difficult behaviors in a child, this was about managing her own difficult feelings about a child she really did not want to raise. So, Patty retreated and did not bring the subject up again with anyone. Accepting that this was her fault, and not the child's, did not help the feelings to go away.

Recently, Patty found herself questioning how she was going to get through the next few years with Donelda. She could manage now, but she had enough experience to know that the small issues that currently existed were going to get much larger when the child entered her teens. "Why did Donelda have to be part of this family? How am I going to be a mother to someone I can't stand to be around?"

Managing the "Oops Response"

With work, it's possible to manage the "oops response" and improve your relationship with your child. The following techniques can help you in this difficult situation.

On a daily basis, look for the positives. Occasional recollections of the child's positive attributes are not enough. You must consider at least some of the good qualities in your child, every day. Prepare a list of the positives to look at during the times when there is nothing that easily comes to mind.

Try to do one thing alone with the child every week. Parent/child casual contact during the busy week can dwindle to almost nothing if you are not careful. Find one activity that you can do alone with the child on a weekly basis. This can be grocery shopping, walking the dog, or playing a board game. Keep the time of the activity short, activity-focused, and child-centered. This is a time for you to suspend all of the negative feelings and give the child one or two hours of good, loving parenting.

Remember that your child needs, and is entitled to, your love. There are a great many duties and responsibilities that come with adoptive parenting, and the most significant of all is providing the child with a sense of being loved. While this is extremely difficult in cases of emotional mismatch, it is still up to you to do the job.

Behave in a loving manner toward your child. Regardless of your feelings toward your child, you must act as if you love her. This means forcing a note of cheerfulness into your voice when your child approaches; smiling at her first thing in the morning and last thing at night; praising her in a loving manner for things she does well; initiating touch; and refraining from always siding with the siblings against her.

Find support. No matter how embarrassed you may be by your dislike for your child, don't keep the feelings a secret. Find someone to talk with who can support you without supporting your negative feelings. Talk to someone who can validate your frustration and ambivalence without agreeing that the child is not likeable and without adding to the reasons why you shouldn't like her.

Remember that adoption is a lifelong commitment. Parents don't always like each of their birth children to the same degree. They may have favorites, or find that one is easier to raise than another. Still, returning a birth child is not an option. Adoption is the same. Once the commitment is made, there is no backing out. You can't return the child simply because she has personality traits that annoy you or because she is more difficult to raise than you had anticipated.

This may be a phase. Feeling an "oops response" to a child may be a part of the overall adjustment. The behaviors or personality traits that you find challenging in the early years of the adoption may become something that you learn to appreciate or begin to ignore as the family unit becomes more cohesive over time. The addition of an older child will inevitably bring about changes in who you are as a person. If you dislike a child early on, you may find later that your personal growth has allowed you to broaden your appreciation of others and your tolerance for difference.

Own the problem. Like it or not, this is your problem. It's not the child's fault if you feel that she has unpleasant personality traits. Her traits are just a part of who she is, much like the color of her eyes or the shape of her ears. She can't control these traits and shouldn't be expected to do so. It is the adult response that needs correction.

Rephrase your thinking. Instead of thinking "If only she would stop clearing her throat every time she starts to speak," learn to think, "If only I could stop reacting so negatively every time she clears her throat."

Consider your past. Who else in your life has displayed these traits? It may be that they are reminders of someone you did not like in your childhood, or someone who hurt you or committed an injustice at some point in your life. If your dislike of the child mirrors your dislike of someone from your past, consider resolving this issue in therapy. Learn to separate it from the child.

CHAPTER 12

International Adoption

Increasing numbers of adopting parents are making the decision to adopt internationally. According to U.S. government figures, there has been a 250 percent increase in international adoptions in the last decade. In 1999 alone, more than 16,000 children were adopted from other countries.

There are many reasons why people make this choice. Some couples, or singles, have special feelings toward a country—maybe their great-grandparents were originally from that country, they love the country's art, or they have traveled through the country and feel an affinity for it. Others believe that if they adopt kids from a foreign country, they will not have to deal with issues like openness, or birth parents changing their minds. Some seek international adoption because they want to raise a child from a particular racial or ethnic background, or they believe that pregnant women in that country do not drink, so there will be no risk of FAS. Still others decide to adopt from overseas in the belief that they are saving a child from a poor or war-torn nation. A very common reason, too, is the speed at which one can adopt from overseas. Many children, even babies, can be adopted from other countries far more quickly than they can be adopted in your own country.

Risks in International Adoption

There are many risks in all adoptions and in all births; but in international adoption, some issues are a greater problem than others. Problems may include:

- Undiagnosed fetal alcohol syndrome
- Differing medical terms
- Hepatitis B and C
- Post-institutionalization problems
- Unknown or undisclosed sexual and/or physical abuse
- Unknown or undisclosed medical history
- The child's lack of any concept of "family"
- The child's emotional and perhaps unknown legal ties to living siblings or parents
- Attachment problems
- Learning and behavioral delays or challenges

Post-Institutionalization

The care of children differs among cultures; many countries do not have a tradition of family foster care. This means that babies, children, and youth without parents are housed in large orphanages for most of their lives. Think about the warehousing of children in the stories of Charles Dickens and you get the idea. That is not to say that the people who run the institutions do not care about the children. However, years of war, poverty, chronic political upheaval, poor understanding of child development, and differing standards in housing and public safety result in understaffed, overcrowded, poorly run facilities.

Children who have spent time in these places often suffer from a lack of basic emotional, and sometimes even physical, care. "Post-institutionalization" is the term that is used to describe the problems that children develop in these institutions and display when they are adopted.

Characteristics of Post-Institutional Behavior

There are many problems that adopting parents have noticed and reported to researchers in the last few years:

- Attachment disorder, resulting from insufficient nurturing and changing caregivers

- Behavior and learning challenges, sleep disorders, and eating disorders, resulting from chronic malnourishment and abuse

- Premature sense of independence, resulting from always being on her own

- Negative survival skills, such as stealing, hoarding food, a quick temper, and physical aggression

- Apparent helplessness—the inability to open a jar, fear of playing in the yard, inability to zip a jacket

- Depression and anxiety

- Lack of tolerance for frustration

- Speech and language delays

- Predisposition toward overstimulation

- Self-abusive behaviors

It is never possible to predict which children will have any particular set of problems, nor is it possible to know how severe any of these problems will be. However, if your child was in a large institution, expect that she will have problems feeling genuine affection for you in the early days of the adoption, as well as having social and emotional delays. The rate at which she catches up or learns new skills will depend on a combination of factors, including: how intelligent she is; how badly harmed she was before she was adopted; how long she was in the institution; and whether she had any other significant attachments in her life.

If your child was in a country that uses family foster care, she may not have had the kinds of problems that develop from orphanage life, but she may have had terrible life experiences prior to going to the foster home. She may have been abused; she may have had to care for sick parents, younger siblings, or relatives. Now she may recall an emotionally intense relationship with her parents or siblings. Perhaps she was very attached to her foster parents, or she did not like her foster parents at all. There are a number of issues you won't know about until she is able to tell you herself.

The Impact on Your Family

The less that is known about your child, the more prepared you must be to jump on a fast learning curve. You will have to find as many resources as possible to help you identify her basic health needs and move on from there. Your child may require extensive dental work or intensive language training. She may also require extra help in learning to cope with so many adjustments.

You may be surprised at how many things she does not know how to do. She may not know how to play, she may not know how to sleep alone, she may not know how to eat with the family, she may not know how to choose clothing in the morning. Or, she may be very sure that she knows all of that, and insist on continuing to do it the way she did in the orphanage, even if it conflicts with the family schedule and routine. Some of these habits may be culturally based or the result of institutionalization. Changing these will be difficult and will require a great deal of patience and understanding on your part. Your child will be very dependent on you for help to learn how to navigate her way around your home, your community, and your lifestyle. But she may resent this dependence, or, after being left to her own devices for so many years, she may not understand that she can rely on you to help her.

After a lifetime of having every moment of every day determined for them, some children can't think of ways to self-amuse. Rather they become clingy, depending on you to provide them with company and entertainment. This kind of behavior, often mistaken for attachment at the beginning of the placement, can become very frustrating for parents.

Some children have no concept of what it means to have a family. On the video supplied by the agency, they may have said they wanted a family, but after a lifetime in an orphanage, the only thing they really know about family is what they have seen in books or on the occasional video. When you begin acting like a mom or dad, the child may be clueless about what it is you are doing. She may view you as caretakers, and treat you accordingly. She may be charming, sweet, and affectionate to everyone who comes to the house or talks to her in the store, and treat you with indifference. This makes sense. She was taught to be charming to visitors who came to the orphanage, and she learned not to attach to orphanage staff who generally only stayed for a while, then moved on to other work. An international adoption can demand difficult changes from both parents and child, as illustrated by Jillian and Jonah's story.

Life Lesson: A Difficult Adjustment

Jillian had been dragged into the adoption in the first place. Now it was falling apart. She and Jonah had turned to adoption after ten years of infertility treatments, miscarriages, one short-lived marital separation, and two job-related transfers. Once they decided to adopt, this relieved the stress to get pregnant and stabilized the marriage. However, it had taken Jonah some time, and some long midnight conversations to convince Jillian to agree to an international adoption.

"I don't think I can do this, Jonah. I think I can bond with an older child, that's not the problem, but I've watched those shows on TV about the children in orphanages and I don't think I can handle that kind of behavior."

"I've watched those shows too," Jonah replied. "I know they look scary, but the parents on those shows all seemed kind of coldhearted to me. I wouldn't have been able to bond with any of them if I was a kid either. We can do better than that."

"But why can't we adopt a little child from some country that does foster care?" Jillian asked.

"We've been through this a hundred times," Jonah sighed. "I want a child with our same ethnic background. I don't care about the race, but I want a child who comes from where our families came from. After all, that could have been us, living in that kind of poverty, if our grandparents hadn't immigrated when they did. This way, we're giving something back to our own heritage."

"Well, I don't see how we're giving something back if we're taking their children, but I can see your point. If we had given birth to a child, it would have had an eastern European lineage, so if we adopt from there, the child will at least have something in common with us." Jillian knew Jonah had his heart set on adopting from this country, and she didn't want to see him disappointed. After all, Jonah had been so supportive of her during the mood fluctuations and the depressions, all those years they had been trying to get pregnant. "Okay, let's do it," she said.

Jerzy was five and Mariah nine when they came home. They had been great in the orphanage and great on the plane ride home. Both of them slept more than they were awake, and ate without balking at the airline food.

The first month at home had been fine. All of the relatives had been over several times to see the kids. Friends and neighbors had arranged barbecues and welcome-home parties for the new family. Even their church had had a special welcoming lunch. More than half the congregation had shown up with presents and balloons, and lots of other treats for the kids.

But once school started, it all went downhill fast. Jerzy was holding his own in kindergarten, but Jillian was being called to the school on a daily basis to deal with one thing after another with Mariah. First it had been stealing from the other kids' lunches, then it had been refusing to line up for assembly or to come back into the classroom after recess. And at home, Mariah had started having temper tantrums that had turned into rages. Now she was hitting Jillian so hard that she was bruising her. Yesterday, she had even bitten her new mom on the hand when Jillian tried to restrain her from hitting the dog with a large frying pan.

"Oh, Jillian," Jonah said when he came home from work and saw the cut skin and tooth marks on his wife's hand. "I never thought this would happen to us. We're doing fine with Jerzy, but it's crazy with Mariah. I never thought you would get hurt. I really thought we could do this."

"Well, we can't, Jonah. I told you I couldn't handle this kind of behavior and I was right. This is not working."

"But what are we going to do?" Jonah asked. "We can't send her back to the orphanage, and she'll get lost forever if we put her in foster care. What can we do?"

Raising Your Post-Institutionalized Child

Following are some suggestions that may be helpful in raising your child.

Get a complete medical and neurodevelopmental assessment as soon as possible after you return home. Your local adoptive parents' association likely has the name of a pediatrician and a psychologist in your area who specialize in international adoptions. They can do the appropriate testing to let you know what your child is currently capable of on an academic and emotional level, and what medical problems might exist.

Go to a dentist and an optometrist as soon as possible. Children from Third World nations often have never had dental or eye care. They may have difficulty learning because of undetected eyesight or hearing problems. They may also have lived with chronic pain caused by tooth decay for most of their lives, so they no longer know that they can have a pain-free life. Some children act out physical pain and discomfort. You may find that your child has the temperament of an angel, once her tooth abscesses are cleared.

Introduce the rest of the family, one by one, over the first year. All of your friends and relatives may be waiting to meet this child, but you have to be a firm barrier to most of them. Let them get to know the child slowly, over a period of time. Remember, your child may have no concept of family. Suddenly being told she belongs to all of these strangers may overwhelm and confuse her, to the point that she starts to shut down emotionally. If she has never had a significant relationship with one adult, don't expect her to develop relationships with several, before she makes some other adjustments first.

Remember that your child is "in recovery." Your child may be recovering from all the loneliness and deprivation that were part of his life for so many years. He may also have past abuse to deal with, as well as physical problems that must heal. Treat him like you would a person who is physically and emotionally fragile, because *he is.*

Use all of the techniques described in chapter 2 to foster attachment. Since part of your child's problem is likely to be RAD, the techniques described in chapter 2 will be very useful for you, your child, and your family.

Reduce the immediate stimulation of the home. During the first few months of the child's arrival in your home, don't provide him with every toy ever made, no matter how badly you want to. Keep the stimulation to a minimum by bringing in most toys (particularly things like computers, video games, and interactive toys) one at a time, over a period of six months to a year. Your child will be exposed to these things, at the homes of other people and at school, but his home environment should be a place where he can relax, without coping with too much too soon.

Consider home schooling for the first six months to a year. This may delay the rate at which your child acquires your language, but it will also reduce frustration, overstimulation, and culture shock.

Teach your child how to play. Your child may have no idea what to do with a doll or toy truck. She may destroy the toys, or be totally disinterested in them. Sit down and play with her, so she can learn that this is a fun and rewarding way to spend her time

Use all of the techniques described in chapters 2, 3, and 8, related to loss and grief, aggressive and sexualized behavior, and cross-cultural and transracial adoption. Each of these challenges may have touched your child's life at some time. Anything to do with boundaries, with discipline that is not punitive, and with bonding will be helpful to your family in those first few months after your child arrives home.

Learn as much of his language as you can before he comes home to you. He needs to be able to express his basic needs as soon as possible, and certain words and phrases can help you to communicate with him, right from the beginning. Simple things—words for certain foods, the rooms in the house, the kinds of animals you have as pets or livestock—can keep your child from feeling totally isolated by language.

Learn to cook his country's traditional foods, as well as foods that were served in the orphanage. She may not have had many of her country's traditional foods, and the quality and variety of food in the orphanage may have been poor, but the more that you serve her that is familiar the more comforted she will feel.

Be patient about eating. She may be a very picky eater, simply because she has not had an opportunity to try many foods. She may never have had most vegetables. Her palate may be sensitive to foods that have even the smallest amount of spice or sweetness. She may need several months, or even years, before she can eat like you do without feeling some stomach upset.

Be patient about manners. Poor manners may be the result of differing customs, or the result of having to eat as much as he could as quickly as possible, before someone else takes it away. Manners are the slightest problem you will have to deal with, so let them go for the first few months. She will learn what she needs to as she becomes more established in your home.

Remember that your child will not likely have age-appropriate social skills. Her manner of relating to others may be more like that of a two-year-old than a ten-year-old. She will need time, teaching, and role modeling to learn how to interact with you and other people at an age-appropriate level.

Stay away from fun places. For the first few months, avoid all the places you would really like to take your child. Places like theme parks, circuses, and fairs may be overstimulating; she may not understand what to do there if she has not learned how to play. The rides may be too stressful and frightening, until she has had an opportunity to learn how to have fun.

Assess for depression, and consider medication. Many older adopted children go through a stage of depression, due to the culture shock and the loss of familiar surroundings, language, and friends. Depression may also be a part of other conditions, such as attachment disorder or post-traumatic stress disorder. Your pediatrician or child psychiatrist will discuss the pros and cons of medication for your child's depression. It may be best to wait it out, or the depression may be so severe that the child's life is in danger. Either way, your family should consider all factors, then decide if an antidepressant is right for your child.

Keep a routine and structure that are evident to your child. Your child will be used to an unvarying routine that fits within a firm structure. He will need time and help to adjust to an easygoing, spontaneous family life. So, keep a schedule of anticipated events that is broken down daily. Put the calendar where he can see it and refer to it frequently. Try to let him know in advance about any changes in routine. Try to avoid as many spontaneous events as possible. It may take at least a year before your child can handle a reduced routine.

One parent should be home with your child for the first year. Your child needs as few new environments and people to adjust to as possible. If he has to adjust to baby-sitters, to different teachers, to daycare, etc., it may prevent him from adjusting and attaching to you.

Learn some of the standard body language and physical gestures of your child's country. Patting a child on the head may be a show of affection in one country and a sign of disrespect in another. Make sure you know the good nonverbal language and the bad (so you know when your child is being disrespectful to you).

Consider room sharing. Your child may never have spent a night, or even a full hour, alone. If he came from an orphanage, he likely shared his room with many other children, and may have shared his bed with at least one or two others. Even if he came from a country that has foster homes, he may have shared both a room and a bed with other children, or even adults.

You may find that letting him share a bedroom with a safe and responsible older child in your family is helpful for the first few weeks, while he gets used to the change in sleeping arrangements. However, the other child will have to be patient and able to put up with a lot. If sharing a room isn't possible, ask the child if he would like to sleep with the radio and lights on. After all, a quiet room with no distractions can be very frightening to a child.

Explain your feelings to your child. Your child may not realize that you have feelings in response to what she does or says. She may be used to an ever-changing array of staff who were not trained in child care and who had little or no interest in the children in the orphanage. She may be very surprised to find out that your feelings are hurt when she calls you "stupid." Don't whine or complain while you tell her this. Use common communication skills such as "Staci, when you yell at me like that, I feel angry," or "Staci, when you broke my favorite vase on purpose, I felt very sad and hurt," or "Staci, when you hug me, I feel very happy."

Some children will use the feelings you have as a means of hurting you further. They may see your feelings as a point of vulnerability which they can manipulate to control the situation. However, you can remain in control of your responses to the behaviors, while still acknowledging that you have feelings and that your child is part of what creates feelings in you.

Be very clear about rules and expectations. Your child will have been well trained with many rules, but he may not have any experience with people who are around enough to actually enforce the rules. So, let him know what the rules are, right from the beginning, and keep gently reminding him. He has little experience with trustworthy and consistent adults, so you can't expect him to believe that you mean what you say. Be patient with this.

Ask your child if he really wanted to be adopted. While they are in the orphanage most children say that they want to be adopted. But that may really mean that he just wants to get out of the orphanage, or that he wanted to get to America because his best friend was adopted to a couple there and he wants to find him. Your child needs to voice what his choice really would have been. If he says he didn't want to be adopted, don't take it personally. He couldn't possibly have understood what it would mean to leave the orphanage, to leave his country, to live in a family, to learn a new language and new customs. He could not possibly understand what it is to be loved by parents. His answer simply tells you what he fears and what he wishes he had. His answer does not tell you how he will feel *after* he has adjusted and has gained enough maturity to reflect on his life's path.

Don't expect your child to act his age. Your child may never have had enough freedom of choice to function now at an age-appropriate level. And he may be so overwhelmed by his new life that he retreats to a younger age. Use this as a reason to "baby" him and begin to establish attachment. You can help him choose which clothes to wear, which food to eat, which shows to watch, which games to play. You can also help him dress by putting on his sweater or socks.

Speak positively about your child's country of origin. You may have found the country to be charming and exciting, or you may have found it to be cold, inhospitable, and dreary. But you must always refer to it in positive ways, because your child's self-esteem and positive sense of identity are linked to everything that is part of his origins. Even if he says he hated the country, you can acknowledge his feelings without adding your own negative feelings.

CHAPTER 13

False Allegations of Abuse

In the last two decades, there has been a significant increase in the disclosure of physical and sexual abuse of children. This has been a promising step forward in making our homes and our communities a safer place for children. When a disclosure is reported, it is vital that the child-protection authorities begin their investigations as soon as possible, and that they be conducted in a manner that protects and promotes the best interests of the child.

The statistics do not separate out how many reports against parents include reports made by older children against adoptive parents, nor do we know exactly what percentage of these reports turn out to be true and what percentage turn out to be false. But we do know that false allegations do happen.

False Allegations Happen

There are many reasons why a false allegation may be made, either by the child or by someone outside of the family. One of the obvious reasons is that adoptive families who are transracial, or who have a large number of children, stand out in the community. People pay attention to them and know who they are. They often have social workers and other professionals involved with the children, as they go through their difficult years, or as they deal with some of the challenges presented in this book. This can leave your actions open to misinterpretation by the community, who know the family sees counselors all the time, who assume that this is because the adoptive parents have problems. A moment of parental temper that results in a yell made in public can be reported by an onlooker as abuse. Certainly, the parent should not be yelling at the child, not in public or at home. But when typical-looking families have a momentary lapse of good parenting skills, a social worker is rarely told about it. The experience of the adoptive family, however, may be that a onetime yell on a hot Saturday at the supermarket results in a visit by child protection authorities.

Ghosts of the Past

Another reason that this can happen is that the children we adopt often have backgrounds of abuse. The child has a narrow perspective on how the system works, and he may not have witnessed any actual punishment for his real offender(s). He may know that after he reported real abuse, he was moved. So, if your angry, acting-out, unattached twelve-year-old is mad because you won't let him pierce his nose, he may very well decide to report you for abuse. From his limited understanding of the world, the only thing that will happen is that he will go to another family where he will have a better chance at keeping the nose ring. He won't understand that you will experience heartache, public humiliation, the possible removal of your other children, social ostracization, the possible loss of your job, collapse of your marriage, false imprisonment, or a number of other consequences.

Fear

Still another reason a false report may be made is that the child misunderstands something you are doing. Based on her past experience, she may think that the affectionate back rub you gave her was a seductive move, that when you tripped and spilled the tea on her arm, it was not an accident. She may genuinely think you tried to harm her.

Retribution

Some children also have serious mental conditions that lead them to say anything that will get them something they want. Whether they want to be moved, to punish you for grounding them, or to re-create the chaos of their pasts, they will make up or exaggerate an incident, and disclose it to their counselor or teacher, knowing it will be reported to authorities. These children generally have numerous and serious problems that everyone involved with them knows about. They are as much a risk to their counselor who sees them alone in her office as they are to you. However, their report will still have to be investigated.

Confused Memories

Still other children are simply confused about who did what to them. Your child may be in a therapy situation where she tells her therapist about the time she was thrown against the wall. This may have happened before she came to your home, but she cannot really remember anything before you adopted her at age four. All she recalls is the pain and fear that are associated with the incident. Since she cannot recall any other mother, she inserts your face into the memory picture.

The Impact of False Allegations

Allegations of this sort are devastating to the adoptive family. They generally result in the immediate removal of the child making the statement. The other children in your home may be taken to foster care. On a social level, it is almost impossible to keep this kind of news private. As word spreads through your local community, it becomes an endurance test just to go to the local store to buy milk. Having to face peers and neighbors can be more daunting than some parents can handle.

Family members may develop emotional problems as they cope with the accusation. You may find that you go into an intense rage followed by deep depression. Some parents have become suicidal. Others have found that the lingering question of whether the allegation is real has torn their marriage apart. Your family's finances may be drained, as you pay for lawyers to defend you or to guide you through the investigative process. Your other children may turn against the reporting child in a violent or vengeful manner as they see their own lives being upset by what they know is a false allegation.

Family members and friends whom you thought you could always rely on may suddenly disappear as they question whether or not the accusation could be true. The church that you have relied on for so long to help you through normal family crises may suddenly seem too public and too full of staring faces to be a source of strength or solace.

You will also find that you feel you are being treated like a criminal by police, social workers, and others involved in the investigative process. They will be treating you either in a neutral manner, or in a hostile manner, but they won't treat you in the friendly way you are used to being treated by authorities. It's hard to get used to being treated like a "bad guy" when you have been a law-abiding citizen all of your life. Jefferson and Margarite's story will help you understand the initial shock of facing such an allegation.

Life Lesson: Being Cast as the Villain

Jefferson and Margarite were reading the local real-estate paper when the social worker knocked at their door. They were completely unprepared for the sight of two intimidating police officers and a woman who identified herself as a child protection investigator.

"You can't be serious?" Jefferson kept repeating. "I would never touch my daughter or any child!"

"Well, we took a credible statement from your daughter, sir," the taller of the two police officers responded. "We can start with your statement here or do the whole thing at the police station. In other words, you can have this the easy way or the hard way. It's up to you."

"We can't go to the police station now," Margarite interjected. "Cleone will be home from school in ten minutes. She can't come home to an empty house."

"Cleone won't be coming home today, Mrs. Williams," said the social worker. "We have taken her into our care and she will be staying in a foster home. I'm here to get her clothes. The courts will determine what to do with her until the accuracy of her statement is determined. In the meantime, you can't have any contact with her. "

"What exactly did she say I did to her?" Jefferson demanded.

"Why do you ask that, sir?" the smaller cop asked as he took out his notebook.

"Why do you think I asked? I want to know what I am charged with!"

"You aren't charged with anything, at the moment. We'll decide that at the police station and you will be informed then. At this time, we have a credible statement that you sexually abused a minor in your home, and that you, Mrs. Williams, knew of this and failed to protect her."

"What?" was all Margarite could say as the tears flooded her eyes.

"I never did anything of the sort!" Jefferson could feel the heat of his anger rushing to his face. They had only had Cleone for a year, and it had been a rough year. There had been times when he had wanted to swat her, but he never did. And he had certainly never thought about her in a sexual way. "She's only nine years old, for God's sake. She's a child. She doesn't even act like a nine-year-old. She's been in an orphanage all her life. She acts like she's four!" he yelled.

"That's what makes this a crime, sir. Now, I recommend you two get your jackets and come with us. We obviously aren't going to get anywhere here, so it's time we head to the station."

"Jefferson, we need to call a lawyer," Margarite managed to say.

"What lawyer?" Jefferson was still yelling. "We've never had a lawyer for anything in our life. Who do we call? What do we do?"

Dealing with False Allegations

Adults who deal with older adopted children should educate themselves to the risk of false accusations and how to deal with them. The techniques below should help.

Find out as much as possible about your child's previous experiences of abuse. The more that you know, the better able you will be to establish firm boundaries in the home and seek the help your child needs now to help her resolve her confusion and trauma, and to reduce the likelihood that she will make a false allegation.

Educate the service providers who work with her. Give them a copy of this chapter, or anything else that explains the risk of false allegations, so that if an accusation should occur, they will realize that this is not an uncommon problem.

Remember, your child may have reported real abuse in the past and then nothing happened. So if an accusation leads to your arrest, she may be as surprised as you that her false report has led to all the uproar and problems. She may have thought she would just get some extra attention from a favorite therapist or teacher, and had no idea that you would be in trouble.

Have a plan. Now that you know it could happen, have a plan for what you will do, who you will call, and what you will say to others, if a false accusation does occur.

Be clear about boundaries. If you adopt an older child, be clear with her, and every member of the family, about your expectations: You expect everyone to be dressed, in pajamas or a robe outside of the bedroom; you do not share bathroom times; bathroom doors are always closed when someone is in the bathroom; you do not change clothes in front of your children; the parent of the opposite sex will not watch the older children change clothes; adults never lie down with a child on her bed; parents do not close a child's bedroom door if they are in the same bedroom with the child; one parent does not stay home overnight alone with an older child until the child has been in the home at least a year.

Explain the "family bed." Do not use the family bed suggestions given in chapter 2 if the child has a history of false reports, or if the child has been sexually intrusive or sexually abused and recently placed with you. If you are using the family bed suggestions, make sure that both parents are present and that everyone has all their clothes on (shoes and socks can be off for a clearly stated purpose, such as doing the "feet" technique). Keep the bedroom door open. Talk to the child's therapist about this technique and why you do it. Make sure that the child understands why you do this and seems comfortable and doesn't seem shy or to be participating just to please you.

Allow the police to search your house. Your lawyer will advise you about whether the police should have a warrant before entering your home. However, if they have the correct papers, do not obstruct their search.

Call a support person right away. Your adoptive parent's support group, or foster parent group, should have support people available for this kind of event. Call that person immediately, so you don't begin to isolate yourself.

Know the name of a lawyer to call. Don't waste time going through the phone book at the police station. Find out now who would be the best lawyer in town to call in case of this kind of problem.

Consult with a lawyer now. Have a onetime meeting with a lawyer to become fully informed on what you should do if this circumstance arises.

Forgive your child. As angry as you may get, you need to understand that she likely did not understand what this would do to your life, so she cannot be held fully accountable for all that happens.

Find out who actually made the allegation. Sometimes an overzealous or undertrained counselor, therapist, or teacher may misinterpret what the child is saying about the family life, and file a report. It may be that the child doesn't even understand what was alleged.

Find out what exactly was alleged. You need to know the exact wording of the accusation. It may be that the charge is "sexual assault," but the alleged act only involved the child seeing Dad naked. You recall this happened accidentally, when you were changing out of your swimming trunks in the tent while you were camping.

Remember, children who do not have permanent families are at high risk of abuse. Children from foreign orphanages, and children who have been in different caregiving situations, are at high risk of being exploited and abused. You will feel like your life has been ruined by a false allegation, but society has to act in a manner to protect the children. You are not paying the price for what the child has said, you are paying the price for society's failure to protect the child in the past.

After It's Over

Assuming that you have been cleared and the incident is behind you, the really hard work will begin. Now you must find a way to put your family back together. For some parents, the answer is to place the child in foster care and give up guardianship. This may be the only route in cases where the child shows no remorse and is at high risk to do this again. However, those situations do not always happen. More likely, the child is remorseful, understands what she has done and what she has lost, and wants some kind of relationship with you.

Whether you take the child back into your home is not a decision to make alone. Involve a number of people working as a team: your therapist, the child's therapist, your lawyer, the social workers, the other children in the family, your spouse, and your extended family.

There will also be a number of factors to consider. Is the child remorseful? Did she make the allegation out of spite or did she make it because she misunderstood your actions? Does the child understand the seriousness of what she did? Maybe it wasn't the child who made the allegation. Maybe it was an adult who misunderstood what the child was saying about your family life. Therapy is essential to dealing with such an allegation. So is forgiveness—from you, from siblings, and from extended family. Before accepting the child back into your home, be sure you have the trust of your spouse and work together to ensure better boundaries and effective communications. Communication is important not only within the family, but also with others who deal with your child regularly, including teachers, therapists, and social service workers.

CHAPTER 14

Play

It is surprising how many waiting children, whether they come from poverty-ridden orphanages in other countries, or excellent foster care in your own community, do not know how to play. Children from other countries may never have had an opportunity to play. There may have not been any toys in the orphanage, or maybe only the biggest and toughest children had access to the few toys that were around. There may have been no age-appropriate toys, or the selection may have been too small to hold their attention. Some children have never been alone, and have not learned to use play as a means of self-soothing or as a means of enjoyment.

A child from your own community may have moved too often to have any toys he could claim as his own, as hurried packing and multiple moves saw toy after toy left behind. Or he may never have been in one foster home long enough to enjoy birthday parties and holiday festivities that usually generate toys for children. Foster parents are usually given money for clothes and food for each child, but not for toys. There may be lovely, expensive toys in the foster home, but the toys stay in the home for each set of children to use while they are there.

Children who become used to passing through home after home soon learn not to spend much time with any particular toy to avoid getting attached to a favorite doll or action figure. A child may develop a pattern of breaking a toy, as soon as he starts to like it. That is his only way of ensuring that he does not feel sad when he has to leave it behind, and that other children don't get to take it. This kind of behavior is rarely seen as a coping skill. Instead, it's misunderstood as destructive and aggressive, and the child is labeled as one on whom it's not worth spending toy money.

Your child may never have learned how to share or to play with another child. Since he doesn't know the rules of play, other children quickly learn to leave him out of games and play situations. With few opportunities for appropriate peer interaction, his social skill development is slowed, and he's at risk for developing secondary problems.

Don't underestimate the importance of child's play. It exists in all cultures and the developmental progress of play is similar from one country to another. Play allows children to explore the world in a safe and controlled manner. It lays the groundwork for developing relationships and builds social skills. Children at play develop their minds. They try new ideas and develop their creativity and problem-solving skills. Play also helps children learn to soothe themselves without turning to an adult for comfort. Learning to release stress and frustration and have fun is a skill that will be invaluable in adulthood.

How Play Skills Impact Your Family

If your child arrives in your home not knowing how to play, he may need you to be his entertainment center. That's fine at the beginning, but even the most selfless parents need breathing space after a few weeks. You want him to find friends, to be able to entertain himself for a half hour here or there, and to find ways to explore his creativity.

When an older child is first adopted, most friends and family, as well as you, will buy the child numerous toys to make him feel cared for and to give him the material goods that are common in our society. However, if he breaks everything within two hours of receiving it, or if he just looks at it, then walks away, you may begin to feel resentful. Other siblings know there would be big trouble if they broke all of their toys, yet you seem to keep buying them for the new kid, even though she's broken everything you've given her. Ken and Laura's story will help you understand how difficult it can be to cope with a child who hasn't learned the value of toys.

Life Lesson: Just Stupid Toys

Ken and Laura had always bought their children the best toys and loved doing so. Watching Tom and Jules' eyes light up as they opened a package, and watching how they cherished some toys and shared or argued over others, was part of the fun of giving. When they met Joseph, they knew he would be fun to buy for as well. They were not well-to-do people, but they had enough to raise their children, and they always spent carefully and budgeted well. By giving up a few dinners out, and cutting short their summer holiday last year, they were able to save enough to have all new bedroom furniture waiting for eight-year-old Joseph, as well as shelves stocked with toys that Tom and Jules helped to pick out. However, within two weeks of Joseph's arrival, not a toy was left. And just as bad, he had broken half of his new brothers' toys as well; and he showed no sign of remorse or conscience. Ken and Laura were astounded.

"What is the matter with you?" Laura asked Joseph. He stood staring at her with those large, soft eyes that usually melted her heart. "Answer me, Joseph." Laura was trying to calm herself and search for words that were less blaming. "Is there something wrong with your toys or are you mad at your brothers or me? Is that why you break everything?"

"I don't know," Joseph muttered. "They were just stupid toys anyway."

"Stupid toys," Laura repeated Joseph's words. "Joseph, they aren't stupid. They are very popular toys with the other kids, not to mention expensive. I need to understand why you ripped the arms off all the action figures. You know Tom was collecting that whole set."

Joseph continued to stare at Laura but said nothing, letting the scowl on his face serve as his answer.

"I'm fed up with this," Laura said to Ken that night after the boys were in bed. "I know he doesn't have a lot of experience with toys, but he has the boys to show him how to play, and we got him so much. Now it's all gone."

"I don't get it either. We've bought him more in the last two months than we bought the other two boys all last year. They're jealous and angry, and they're beginning to resent Joseph. I thought having three boys that were about the same age would be great, but Joseph is turning out to be a real fly in the ointment."

"Well, he isn't that bad, Ken. I mean he's real clingy to me and to you and it's starting to drive me nuts. But he's also sweet and affectionate and I think there are times when the boys really like him. I know he just about worships Jules."

"You're right. He's got a lot of really good things about him. I'm not talking about not finalizing the adoption, but we've got some real problems here. Christmas is only two months away, and I'm already feeling resentful when I think about how much we spend on the kids for presents. I know that Joseph will break everything before New Year's."

"Oh, Ken, when did everything start to be about money?"

"This isn't just about money, Laura, this is also about protecting things that belong to our other sons, and teaching Joseph to respect things that belong to other people."

Helping Your Child Learn to Play

Play is an important skill for your child to develop, and a difficult skill for older children to master. You may need to take an active role in teaching your child to play. The following tips will help.

Don't take broken or rejected toys as a sign that he is rejecting you. He may break toys so that he doesn't get attached to them or because that's all he's ever known to do with toys. He may not understand how to use them and becomes frustrated because they are too difficult for him. Some toys he may reject as too babyish, because he is embarrassed that he doesn't know what to do with them. Other toys may be associated with a bad or painful memory. It is unlikely that you will ever know exactly why your child is breaking or rejecting toys. It's not a rejection of you; it's simply a result of deprivation.

Buy toys that are suitable for a variety of ages. Your child will likely want to play with toys that are more appropriate for a much younger child. This is normal and is important because it helps the child to "grow up" through play.

Play little-child games with your child. The standard games that use body language along with words are excellent for helping your child learn to interact with others while playing. Games such as "Ring Around the Rosie" and songs such as "Itsy Bitsy Spider" will help with this. Try these even if the child is a teen. You can do them in a silly, playful manner, so the child or teen doesn't feel like a "baby," but rather sees the game as a means for the two of you to joke around and have fun together.

Teach your child how to play with toys you buy. When you give your child a new toy, sit down with him and help him put it together, or help him figure out how to play with it. Show your daughter how to change the clothes on her doll, or show your son how to use the action figures. Play simple board games with her and gradually increase the complexity and age level needed to play the game. This will reinforce her academic skills and give you more ways to be together.

Play with your child in the house. Make tent cities with her in the living room. Have a pillow fight night, or play board games and card games that help her to expand her concentration and attention span.

Play with your child outside. Climb a tree with her at the park, swing on a swing, play tag in the backyard, go skating, or play water volley ball at the local pool. These activities let her learn to use her large muscles for play and give the two of you opportunities to bond.

Don't give her too many toys at once. Have a few basic toys for when she moves in, then add to them over the next few months. This will keep her from getting overwhelmed, and will keep you from getting mad if she only breaks a few rather than several hundred dollars' worth in a week.

Buy toys for both genders. They may be "all girl" or "all boy," but children need to experience toys that are generally played with by the other gender so they can develop their creativity and expand their imagination.

For the first few months, focus on toys that use the large muscles. Toys and games that let her run, sweat, and get tired will allow her to expend some of her nervous energy and release the tension and stress that are building in her body as she tries to adjust to her new life.

Pair her up with another older adopted child. Other children who can recall going through the same adjustment period of adoption can be a tremendous help in teaching her how to play. You do not have to do this formally, just get them together and let the natural interactions between the children occur.

Let your child watch TV shows designed for younger children. Television can show her ways of playing that she hasn't noticed before. She may see some of the same toys or games, such as dress-up, that you try to play with her. Younger-age shows will be appropriate because they are more likely to meet her emotional age than are shows that are designed for her age group. Don't force her to watch the show, just put it on, or casually tell her you really like a certain show, and ask if she would like to watch it with you. If you have a TV in the kitchen, put it on while you are cooking and ask her if she would like to help you while you peel carrots. This allows her to casually watch the show without admitting that she likes "little kid stuff."

Be patient. The newly adopted older child has a world of things to learn. Be patient while she learns to play without breaking things.

Simulate baby play at the pool. When you are at the local pool, try gently splashing water on his chest or arms. This is the kind of thing parents do with infants while they are bathing them and is a precursor to real play.

CHAPTER 15

Can I Get a Little Respect Here?

When you adopt an older child, you may find that your life is suddenly filled with service providers. There may be learning assistants or language assistants in the classroom, as well as teachers. There may be social workers and family therapists and child therapists and psychologists and psychiatrists. And there may be more dental visits than you ever imagined possible.

You may find that people you do not know behave as if they know you. Word gets out about families who make different choices, even in big cities. When you adopt an older child, suddenly everyone you encounter begins to take an interest in your family. You may find that some of these people, maybe the child's therapist or your favorite bank teller, begin to act as if they have some claim on your child. You may even find that the friendly grocery store clerk ignores your role as mom, and is starting to act as if she has some kind of "special" connection with your child. Some people may view your older child as public property. They know he did not "belong" to anyone before, and they do not recognize that now he "belongs" to you.

The lack of respect, or credibility, given to adoptive families is not the result of people trying to be mean. Generally, people behave this way because society in general does not always respect the adoptive connection as having the same meaning as the genetic connection. They see your family as being more like a foster family than a birth family. They may see your child as an "orphan," even after the adoption has been finalized.

These well-meaning people have watched countless television shows about the plight of children from other countries, or they have read about a child who was beaten by her foster mother (and not read about the hundreds of thousands who are not beaten in foster homes), and believe that the child somehow needs them in his life. What they don't recognize is that the child has already been "rescued" by you, and that the child now has a committed and stable family that is quite capable of taking care of him.

How Disrespect Impacts Your Family

When people do not understand that their attempts to connect with the child only serve to widen the gulf between you, to undermine your claim to parenthood, they unwittingly treat your adoptive affiliation with disrespect, and slow the bonding process and your attempts to establish a family identity.

Service providers, such as therapists or dentists, who do this sometimes do not have adoption-sensitive training, and do not understand that you have to be the most important person in your child's life. When they try to take that place, they are becoming obstacles to your bonding and to your attempt to form a new family identity. When strangers, such as store clerks or other mothers in the park, try to do this, they are often seeing your child as public property, and don't understand that you are capable of taking care of your child without their interference. These people can reduce your child's ability to see you and your spouse as his primary caregivers. He may feel that others are acting this way because they know something about you that he doesn't, or their attentions may lead him to suspect that this is just another temporary living situation. He may have only limited bonding capacity when he first moves into your home, and if someone else claims that bond, he may feel that he can't risk becoming attached to you, in case the other person should take him.

Your child may begin to feel embarrassed to be seen with you in public, because he thinks that the attention he is getting is because of something strange about you. Or he may not want you to stay with him at the therapist's office, because he can't stand the emotional strain of conflicting loyalties he experiences whenever you and the therapist begin to play emotional tug-of-war over him. Sam's experiences illustrate how people outside the family can intrude on your developing relationship with your child.

Life Lesson: This Is My Daughter

Sam had waited to become a father for fifteen years. When he was younger, he had not wanted to get married until he had his career established. When he had his career established, he found that there was no one around he wanted to marry. He knew that it would happen someday, but he was afraid that by then, he would be too old to be a father. When Sam realized that he could adopt as a single man, he went for it. And when four-year-old Sarah Lynn was placed with him, he was ecstatic. He took extended parental leave from his company and arranged a work-at-home schedule for when he went back. Before he knew it, a year had passed.

And it had been the best year of his life. His days began with a big hug and happy grin from his little girl, and ended with her falling asleep in his arms as he read her a bedtime story. He had learned to check the water before putting her in the tub; he had learned to make the tastiest porridge in town; and he could bake cookies while working on her trike and singing along with the dancing dinosaur on TV. Sarah Lynn's growth, her blossoming vocabulary, and her cheerful personality told Sam it had been the best year of her life, too. No doubt about it, they were a team. At least they were in the house. But once they set foot out the door, that was another matter.

"How's my cute little Sarah Lynn?" the receptionist gushed when they entered the pediatrician's office for her routine checkup.

"My little Sarah Lynn is just fine," Sam replied. "Is the doctor on schedule today?" he asked, trying to get the receptionist to focus back on her work.

"Oh no, he's behind as always," she said. "Here, why don't you hand her over, and I'll see if I have a special treat for this little girl." The woman's arms were reaching out through the glass partition above her desk like an octopus emerging from a rock.

"Oh, I'm fine with her," Sam said, pulling back. "We'll just find a storybook to read while we wait." He could feel Sarah Lynn's arms tightening around his neck. Evidentally, she was not too keen on Octopus Lady either.

"Don't be silly. She'll just get bored and fidgety. Besides, we have a new nurse working here, and I promised her I'd show her our little Sarah Lynn when she came in."

"Our little Sarah Lynn?" Sam repeated, still backing away from those sinuous-looking arms.

"Well, we think of her as our own little girl. After all, we see her every month, don't we?" The receptionist had pulled herself back to her side of the partition. "I'll just come around through the door and get her, that way you won't drop her over my desk."

"Oh, my gosh. I just remembered. I have an important appointment of my own to get to, and if the doctor is going to be late, I'll never make it," Sam said. "I'll just leave and reschedule another time."

"Well, you can't do that. Your medical plan doesn't cover missed appointments." The receptionist stopped in her tracks.

"That's okay, just bill me," Sam said as he walked hurriedly out the door.

"I don't like that lady, Daddy. She scary." Sarah Lynn held tight to Sam's hand as he put her down so that she could walk on the sidewalk.

"I know, honey. Daddy isn't so keen on her either," Sam replied. He felt like he'd just escaped something dangerous. "Why don't we go get an ice cream? We have lots of time."

They crossed the street to the fast-food outlet that Sam occasionally took Sarah Lynn to when he was too tired to cook.

"Well, there's my favorite little girl," said the shift manager. He was barely more than a kid, Sam observed. The young man laid aside the broom he was using to sweep the floor. "Have you missed me, Half-Pint? I bet you have." He went on, without waiting for an answer. "So, Daddy won't cook again today, hey. Well, lucky you have me to get you some food." The young man grinned at Sarah Lynn. She shrank against Sam's leg and pulled at his jacket as if to cover her face from the shark-like teeth of the manager.

Getting Respect for Adoptive Relationships

There are a variety of ways to tell the world, "This is my child and we are a family." The suggestions below can help you convey this very important message and increase your child's sense of belonging.

Consider your own values about adoption. Do you consider adoption to be a "second choice"? Do you believe that adoptive families are not as "real" as birth families? Do you believe you are raising another person's child? These values and beliefs are common in society, and they may have influenced you more than you know. It's important that you feel strong and secure in your role as an adoptive parent, so that when you challenge those who are disrespectful of your family ties, you do so knowing in your heart that your family has value and worth, and is as "real" as a family formed by birth.

Claim your child. It's important that you know in your heart that your older child is in fact your child, and that you, and only you, are the mother and father to this child. There may be birth parents, foster parents, and extended family in your child's life, but you are the only one who will raise the child, and this is the only child that will have this particular place in your heart and in your life.

Tell people to back off. There may be times when you have to stand up and tell people that they are interfering in your family. This isn't easy, especially when these people are well-meaning. However, your child needs to understand how important she is to you, and if she feels that you are not keeping her firmly within the boundary of your family, then she will begin to get insecure. For example, when someone refers to your child with inappropriate terms of affection, you can say, "I'll bet you wish you had one just like her. But lucky for me, Sarah Lynn is my little girl." Or you may have to be confrontational, such as "I appreciate your intentions, but I don't feel comfortable when someone else calls my daughter by that term."

Announce the adoption in the local newspaper and in your adoptive parents' association newsletter and church newsletter. You may not be able to do this in cases where you have to protect the identity of your child; however, that is rare. An ad in the papers that proclaims your relationship to this child is a public statement that can hold back many interfering others.

Have a claiming ceremony in your church. A claiming ceremony is a celebration in which the child is acknowledged to have become part of the family. This means telling the community that you are a family and gives formal, public recognition to your relationship with your child. Some churches have a form of this, others do not, but most are willing to help any family gain recognition and to welcome a child into the life of the church.

Act like a family. If you haven't had your child with you very long, you may hesitate to touch him in public. But it's important that you do the casual touching that is normal in families as soon as possible. Hold his hand when crossing the street, touch his shoulder when you are waiting in line at the movies, give him a spontaneous bear hug when he knocks the pins down while bowling, smooth his hair when you get out of the car to go shopping, or straighten his jacket while you are walking in the store aisles. These are all means of proclaiming to the world that this is your child.

Dress alike. Even most teens will not object if you have matching vests to wear when you are out in the winter. Or, with younger children, you can buy jackets that are the same color, hats that match, or wear clothes with some kind of insignia such as a simple animal or tree symbol that you can sew on the sleeve of your coats. These will all help to identify you to the world as members of the same family.

Refer to the child as "my daughter" rather than by name. When you are around people who disrespect your family unit, reinforce your relationship to the child by referring to her as your daughter rather than by her name. That can serve as a nonconfrontational reminder to others.

Provide an in-service on adoptive family relationships. If your family relationships are not being respected by a major service provider, such as a center that provides you with speech therapy or physical therapy, then offer to provide an in-service training to employees at one of their staff meetings. If you do not feel that you can do this, arrange for someone from your local adoptive parents' association or a local adoption social worker to do this.

Support your other children as your family re-forms. Your children may have peers who do not consider the new, older child to be their "real" sibling. Your other children may need you to help them practice what to say when a peer says, "So, who's the new kid at your house?" or "How can he be your brother when he's older than you?" or "My parents say that your family is weird because you and your brother are different colors."

CHAPTER 16

Maintaining Your Married or Single Lifestyle

Most new parents go through a stage when their life is in upheaval from nighttime feedings, disrupted sleep patterns, and a new focus on the baby. When you adopt a baby, you know that you and your spouse can at least have time for coffee together while the baby naps in the afternoon, but when you adopt an older child, you may suddenly find yourself without any privacy. You may discover that this child stays up as late as you do. And, if she is still in the clingy stage, she won't leave you alone for a single minute. On the other hand, if she is presenting behavioral challenges, you won't be able to leave her alone for a minute.

Adapting to a new child, no matter what the age when she arrives, can be exhausting. The entire process takes up your days and becomes a point of high drama. You likely spent several months, if not years, talking about older-child adoption before you even applied. Once you began the home study, your life became centered around the process of getting your child. Then, the big moment came when you got to meet her, followed by the excitement of the pre-placement visits, and then the final arrival. All this stress, albeit positive, takes a toll. Instead of having time to rest and re-energize, you find that with the arrival of your child, you face a new level of activity and demands on your time and energy.

New Demands

Even experienced adoptive couples find that they begin to lose sight of each other as the family adapts and transforms. The needs of the children are generally paramount. Also, since older children often require the help of support services and counseling for the first year, you might suddenly find that you have to be in ten places at once, every day, just to take care of the basics. If your child comes from another country, you may be learning a new language or learning to cook new types of food. You may also be juggling job-related responsibilities and finding that things aren't working out as smoothly as you had anticipated.

Siblings who were already in the home may not be adjusting well to the new child so the level of tension there increases, as well as the demands that you spend your time playing referee. You may find that you have to quickly develop and teach conflict resolution skills, and find the time to make sure the children use them.

The Impact on Your Family

A strong relationship between the parents is the foundation of a family. When you adopt an older child, the stresses and challenges will chip away at any existing weaknesses. As a result, a relationship that could have limped along for several more years may suddenly become unstable. Your older child and other family members will realize something is amiss. If your older child is still at the stage of trying to gain control by undermining the parents as a couple, then she will exploit this weakness to manipulate the family system. This isn't because she's mean or spiteful. She's simply trying to survive by using familiar strategies.

If the marriage is unable to withstand these problems, then it will dissolve. For the couple, this brings all the things that accompany divorce—heartbreak, distrust, division of assets, loss of income, loss of self-esteem, and personal upheaval. For your older adopted child, it may mean the loss of any chance she had to resolve and recover from her past, and establish a new life in a healthy and functional manner. She may know that she was the final factor in the end of the marriage and feel tremendous guilt.

For Couples

The demands of acclimatizing a new child to your family use up the limited time you had in your day prior to the child's arrival. As the child's challenges begin to surface, you may find that you and your spouse are not in agreement over how best to respond to the child. Even couples who have successfully parented other children together can find that the new child pulls them in different directions, around issues such as discipline or consistency of approach. Your exhaustion and child-centered focus may leave you irritable and crabby with your spouse. Little things that you never noticed about your partner before may now be large issues that quickly bring you to the boiling point. And the lack of time that you have together may have caused you to drift apart. Cracks that already existed in your marriage may become giant gulfs between the two of you. Or, if your child presents challenges that require both of you to be present most of the time, you may find that the two of you are forced to be together more than you like. The little escapes, like the time at the gym, may no longer be possible. As Tony and Andrea's story shows, even a fairly long, stable marriage can be strained by the demands of adoption.

Life Lesson: Make Marriage the Priority

Tony and Andrea had been married fifteen years by the time they became parents. They had been through some rough times, but had managed to work things out so that now they had a comfortable life together that let each of them maintain some personal freedom, yet allowed them to enjoy their marriage.

And then, along came seven-year-old Lisa Jo. She was full of energy and kept them going from morning till night. Tony and Andrea both liked the way she brought them into contact with the world of children and they delighted in getting reacquainted with things through her eyes. For two years, they had a good time taking her places, going on mini-vacations, visiting the grandparents, and getting ready for school after summer break. At least the time that revolved around Lisa Jo had been good. However, something wasn't right between the two of them anymore.

"You're always crabbing at me for something, Andrea. Can't you just let me finish working on this bed?"

"You spend your life in this shop, Tony. I never see you anymore after dinner."

"What do you mean you never see me?" Tony put down the level and looked at his wife. "I'm usually either here, making toys and furniture for Lisa Jo, or I'm reading to her or helping with her bath. I might actually go out of the house alone to mow the lawn, but I guess it's too hard for my family to get by while I'm gone, especially if I stay outside to trim the hedge," he said, not trying to hide the sarcasm in his voice.

"I don't need this from you, Tony," Andrea replied.

"Yeah? Well, what do you need from me?" Tony stood up and leaned against the bunk he had just set in place. "All you ever want from me is another piece of furniture to match the dollhouse you've made out of Lisa Jo's room. Or you need me to watch her while you go out with the girls once a week. Or you need me to work overtime so I can get a promotion so we can afford another child. Of course, the fact that I'd prefer to be at home with my little girl, rather than sitting at work listening to my arteries harden, isn't important to you, is it?"

"This is getting out of hand, Tony." Andrea was mad, too. "All I said was that you spend too much time in your workshop. I don't see you in the evenings anymore. By the time you come to bed, I'm asleep. Which is the way I'm beginning to think you want it to be."

"What is that supposed to mean?"

"Let's put it this way. You're a good dad. In fact, you're a great dad. But you aren't much of a husband anymore."

Tony threw down the rag he had used to wipe his hands. "And who am I supposed to be a husband to?" he shouted. "You aren't around anymore either. You're always on some committee meeting at Lisa Jo's school, or you're making her costumes for her skating-club performance, or you're rushing off to some save-the-earth gathering because you've suddenly become an earth mother and you have to single-handedly make sure our daughter has clean air to breathe when she grows up. And then, of course, there's all the therapy and dental appointments you take her to on weekends and after school."

"Those things are part of being a parent, Tony." Andrea had to remind herself not to clench her teeth as she sought to control her anger. "We had a lifetime of doing things for just us. Now I have this beautiful little girl and I want to be a part of her life. I want to make sure she goes to a school that has enough computers and a safe playground, and I want to make the costumes she wears so that she looks pretty and, when she grows up, she'll have special memories of me. And what's so bad about wanting her to have clean air to breathe?"

Tony was silent for a moment, and then took a deep breath before he spoke. "Nothing is wrong with those things. But what about what I'm doing? I'm not out in a bar or running around with other women. I'm here in my workshop making my little girl the bedroom of her dreams. I want her to have memories of me, too. What's wrong with that?"

"Nothing," Andrea admitted. "There's nothing wrong with what either of us is doing."

"So, what's wrong with us?" Tony asked.

Maintaining and Enhancing Your Relationship

It's difficult to juggle responsibilities to your children and your relationship with your mate, but remember—your marriage is the most essential element of your family life. With care, your marriage should last long after your children leave the nest. Try the following helpful hints.

Make your relationship with your spouse the priority in the family. Your marriage is the foundation of your family. The family needs you to stay together as a couple and to be happy with each other. The children need to see healthy adult relationships, and you are the best and most important role models.

Establish a date night. If you do not already have a weekly date night, begin the routine now. It does not matter what you do. Go out to dinner and a movie; go for a walk around the local park; go for a long bike ride together and finish it up with a picnic; rent a hotel room and enjoy three intimate hours alone, without anyone other than room service knocking on the door; get together with friends; join a bowling team as a couple; take a community education course; work out at the gym and follow it up with a long swim. The only rules are that you spend time together and leave the children with the sitter.

Take respite away from home. Most domestic adoptions of older children have some kind of subsidy provided. Try to negotiate respite for at least four weekends a year, so that you and your spouse can go away together. Staying at home may be less expensive, but it allows for too many distractions. Also, it's better for the children to have a sitter come into the home than for them to have to go to the sitter.

Pay attention to your partner's work stress. One or both of you may be working outside of the home. Make sure that you remember to ask your partner what is happening at work. And be supportive of work-related stress. You may be in crisis from being at home all day with a violent and unattached five-year-old, but your partner's work world has not stopped. Your partner is still facing all of the same stresses and demands of work that were present before the adoption; but now, she has to face them with inadequate sleep, no opportunity to relax at home in the evening, and no time to reenergize. You should rub her back, listen to her talk about the contract she just lost, and genuinely care about what is going on in her work day.

Say "I love you" and mean it. At least once a day, look your partner in the eyes and tell her that you love her. And while you are doing so, bring to the front of your mind all the reasons why you fell in love to begin with, and why you have stayed in love for so long.

Compliment each other. At least once a day, say something nice to your partner and remind him that he is an important person in your life.

Play together. Try to find things to do together that are fun. This can be dancing, or it can be some kind of creative craft or hobby. Make sure whatever you choose makes you laugh when you're together.

Tell other people how much you love your partner. Hearing yourself say wonderful things about your partner can reinforce your positive feelings.

Go out with other couples. Socializing with other couples can help you to remember that you are a couple, not just parents.

Use counseling. Don't be afraid to seek help if you find you are drifting apart, or if you find that you are not communicating as well as you used to. Counseling can not only save crumbling marriages, it can also reinforce good ones.

Attend couples retreats. Many churches, community organizations, and professional counseling services offer marriage or couples retreat weekends. These can help you tune up your relationship, strengthen your commitment to each other, and remember why you are in love.

Attend adoption conferences together. It's important that both of you learn how to relate to your child and how to maintain your family. If only one of you goes to these learning venues, then over time, you may find that the partner who is learning the most becomes the in-house expert on all of the challenges. The expert may begin to feel that he or she has all of the responsibilities and is the heavy in parenting duties. This can lead to resentment and anger for both parties.

For Singles

Adopting as a single parent has additional challenges. The time you used to spend with friends, visiting family, or pursuing personal interests, will evaporate as you face the needs presented by the child. If you already have a child in your home when you decide to adopt, you may find that the conflict between the two children means that you can't turn your back on them long enough to get some gardening done or spend more than ten minutes in the grocery store.

If this is your first child, you may have quite a challenge adjusting to never being alone, except when you are in bed or in the bathroom, and even then, you may find your child is always banging on the door, demanding to know when you will be available. The healthy lifestyle you enjoyed for so many years may be curtailed. You'll learn a whole new way of cooking, such as finding fifteen different ways to make macaroni nutritious. The only exercise you'll have time for is running up and down the basement stairs with the never-ending laundry.

Work can also be a problem. You may have prepared for a few weeks or months of parental leave, and then find that your child needs far more than you are able to arrange. Baby-sitting or after-school daycare arrangements may fall through at the last minute, leaving you with no backup and no one else to fix the problem.

Just like couples, you may find that you are exhausted. You may have to watch your child all the time. You may have to stay awake until she sleeps at night. You may have to be sure you get up first to prevent damage to your home or raids on the refrigerator. You may find that you used to sit down and take a minute when you needed to, and now you never sit down unless it's to help your child with homework or to supervise her time-out. Barb's story illustrates the difficulties of adjusting to life as a single parent. Sometimes not being needed is more difficult to cope with than being needed.

Life Lesson: There's More to Life ...

Barb was delighted with being a mother. These last two years had been full of unexpected problems, but she had found that being a mom was filled with even more unexpected joy. Yes, being a mom was all she had ever hoped for, and more. Her twins, Evan and Shawn, had taken some time to adjust to their new life with her, but they had all gone to family therapy for a few months, and now things were working well. The boys had lots of friends in the neighborhood and they had just finished their first year in soccer. Barb was delighted that both boys were showing signs of genuine athletic ability. Barb was going to have to find them some more sports activities to keep them active and see where their talents lay.

She looked around the room. The boys were outside playing, and she had some time on her hands. Now that they were eight, they were more independent than before. Since things were more settled, she could take a breath and look around at her life to see what needed doing next. Barb sat on the living room sofa and sighed. What *did* need doing? The laundry was done, the boys had put the supper dishes in the dishwasher before they went out to play, and she had made their lunches for tomorrow. There was nothing significant happening the following day so it would be the same routine they had established over the last few months. She had three hours before the time she liked to go to bed. She would give the boys a quick bath just before bed, and if they weren't too tired from their busy day, she would read them a story. But they did not need much else from her in the evenings anymore. She was happy that they were so secure and well-behaved, but the chaos of the early days, when they first came to her, had been fun in an odd way, too. At least then, she always had something to do. Something besides sitting around waiting for her boys to need her.

Preserving the Non-Parenting Portion of Your Life

Your children are an important part of your life, but they shouldn't be your whole life. As Barb's story shows, if you become too dependent on your children, your life will feel empty, as they start to mature and find a life outside your home.

Find, and socialize with, other single, adoptive parents. These people can give you tips on how to take care of yourself, and they can become a valued support system.

Keep an interest that is separate from adoption and from your child. Choose one of your favorite pre-child activities and stick with it, regardless of what is going on at home. This will help you to maintain your identity and to remember that there is a life outside of adoption. This is especially important when you are going through the really bad times that can come with some of the challenges.

Build some time into each week that is just for you. Get a sitter and leave the house. Honor your feelings, if it feels like you need time alone. Plan ahead so that you can meet with friends. Go to a movie, either with a friend or alone; go to dinner; go to the gym or for a walk; take a course that's not related to child rearing; go ahead and date someone who interests you.

Don't introduce your date to your child unless the relationship is becoming serious. Your child has had lots of people coming and going in his life, so protect him from the people who come and go through yours. Don't introduce your child to someone you are dating until you feel sure that this is going to be a long-term relationship. Be sure your potential partner has the ability to accept your child as part of the whole package.

Be honest with your child about whether you are dating someone. Older children are very good at understanding what is going on, even if the adults try to hide everything. If you are dating someone, tell the child who it is. If it is casual dating, then explain to the child that you and this person enjoy each other's company and like to do things together, but since it's not serious, your date and your child won't have to meet. If your child insists on meeting the person, then have your date over for a cup of coffee before you go out, but nothing more. Your child may feel the need to actually see the person to determine if he is safe for you, but shouldn't get involved any further.

Have backup care. You probably have people lined up to help you out when your child is sick and you have to go work, and you probably have people to help you when you want to go out. But make sure you have someone who can come in and take over, or can take your child, when *you* are sick. If you never raised children before this one arrived, you will likely find that you catch every cold and flu bug going around your child's school. You'll be ill more days in your first year of parenting than you were in the previous five years. Make sure there is someone who can give you a chance to rest and recuperate when you need it.

Use respite time. You need to go away three or four weekends a year without your child, with someone or on your own. If you go with someone, try to be sure it's someone who won't drain your energy, and can let you do what you need (such as sleep around the clock, instead of hang gliding).

Plan vacations that make you happy, too. It is fun and exciting to have child-centered vacations. But try to build in some vacation time that is fun and exciting for you, as well. If you are staying in a hotel, get one that has baby-sitting services (the hotel should be able to vouch for the safety, screening, and training of the sitter), so you can spend some time in the pool on your own, or have a late-evening dinner in the dress-up lounge instead of a peanut-butter sandwich at the kitchenette counter. If you are going camping, try going to a large, commercial campground that has lots of supervised and structured child activities, so you have some time to yourself while your child does crafts or goes on supervised hikes.

Don't take on too much. Like all new adoptive parents, you have waited a lifetime for this child, and now you want to be involved in all aspects of parenting. However, you only have a limited amount of time and energy, and your child is going to take most of it. So, when the call comes out for volunteers at the school bake sale, keep your hand down. When the school newsletter comes around, pleading with parents to join the parent/teacher association, avoid the recruiters. And you are not letting your son down if you do not become a Scout leader for his pack.

Once the appointments with dentists, doctors, therapists, and social workers have ended, you can begin adding one or two activities that interest you and fit into your life. Volunteering in activities that are part of your child's life is fun, and gives you a means of meeting other parents and staying involved with your child, but choose the one or two that have the most reward for you in terms of your own interests and schedule, and leave the rest for other parents.

Accept offers of help from others. When friends or family offer to baby-sit for free on occasion, take them up on it. If they aren't sincere, they won't offer again. If they are sincere, you may find that you have unexpected opportunities to run out and do some shopping on your own, or get the dog to the vet, without having to take your child.

CHAPTER 17

Avoiding Power Struggles

Power struggles are conflicts that occur when you and your child compete for control of a discussion, situation or event. Typically, children begin to challenge your authority at around age two, when the child learns to say "no." It's easy enough to deal with then. You have the size, experience, physical capacity, and understanding to find any number of ways to either ignore the child's resistance or redirect the child to comply. But power struggles continue to exist between parents and typical children throughout our lives. We have them when the eight-year-old won't wear his jacket to school on a rainy day because "I never get cold." We have them when the twelve-year-old won't wear her glasses at school because "they make me look ugly." We have them when the fourteen-year-old wants to dye her hair pink because "All my favorite rock stars have pink hair." We have them when the eighteen-year-old decides to skip college and go to work at a trendy restaurant, asking "What do I need college for? I'm making $7 an hour." We have them when the twenty-year-old brings home the girl of his dreams. "I know she smokes a little dope, Mom, but it doesn't affect her life at all." Power struggles never end, even in typical families.

In older-child adoption, your child will have larger issues over which to struggle, and he will have more skills in creating and winning power struggles. He may also see every power struggle as a life-or-death situation, which he intends to win, regardless of the cost to himself or to you. Rages, threats, damage to the house, and violence to you or to himself can be the outcome, whether he loses or wins.

Why Power Struggles Become Severe

There are many reasons why your older child engages in such severe power struggles. From past experience, he's learned that when he loses, he gets hurt. He may not know there are ways to handle conflict so that there is no absolute winner or loser. His past role-modeling may have been "win at all costs" rather than "let's see how we can compromise and resolve this situation." This places a lot of responsibility on you. How do you handle conflict? Do you become angry, elusive, or swallow your pride and discuss the situation calmly? Your child may be unable to handle the intensity of feelings he experiences when he is angry at you or you are angry at him, especially if he feels he has a lot at stake. Watching you deal with conflict and anger will help him learn to maintain control of his temper. A therapist can help teach your child anger management skills and can help you explore your own style of conflict management.

The Impact on Your Family

Power struggles are dangerous because they pit the parent against the child, creating a situation in which you and your child are on opposite sides of a situation. The anger and hostility reinforce attachment problems, aggression, the sense of loss, or any of the other challenges we have looked at in this book.

Power struggles polarize not just individuals, but the whole family. Others in the house will begin to take sides on issues, joining you in your fight against the child, or joining the child in his fight against you. Either way, family members become torn by divided loyalties.

Power struggles do not get resolved. The anger and polarization that result from one power struggle can seep into other areas of disagreement, so the atmosphere in the house becomes tense, a fertile ground for more hostilities.

Diffusing Power Struggles

Power struggles are rarely about the issues over which you and your child are fighting. They are more usually about larger issues, such as fear, control, vulnerability, overwhelming change, intense feelings, or unresolved past issues. They may spring from how you were raised and what you thought you could expect from a child. To diffuse a power struggle, you must first do a self-inventory and decide what you need to change in yourself. Then you can look at the communication pattern between you and your child. You can use conflict resolution skills to transform the power struggles into opportunities for negotiation. Kay and Shayla's story shows us how in a conflict, communications can grind to a halt.

Life Lesson: Avoid the Argument

Kay knew that there was going to be a problem tonight. Six-year-old Shayla had been edgy ever since supper. First, she had picked at her vegetables and complained that the meat was too hard and hurt her teeth.

"It's chicken, Shayla. It can't get too hard," Kay had said.

"It's hard to me. It makes my teeth hurt and my mouth gets tired when I chew on it," Shayla pouted.

"It's chicken, Shayla. Chicken can't make your mouth tired, and there's nothing wrong with your teeth," Kay replied.

Shayla continued to dawdle over the meal, finally dumping the large amount of remains into the sink with her dish. The loud clink of the dish hitting the enamel let Kay know that Shayla would not have been upset had the dish broken.

"Why don't you go play outside?" Kay suggested, hoping a little outside play would help Shayla get into a better mood. As she wiped down the table and counter tops, she tried to figure out what was upsetting Shayla. The teacher had reported a good day at school, and Shayla had seemed cheerful at swimming lessons. It had started during dinner. One minute Shayla had been fine, the next she was obviously moving into one of her moods.

Kay startled at the sound of the dog yelping. She ran to the door to find the dog cowering by the gate and Shayla riding her bike across the lawn. "You ran over the dog's tail again, didn't you, Shayla?"

"I don't know, I wasn't looking." Shayla continued to ride the bike in large circles around the perimeter of the lawn. The dog cowered against the gate post each time the bike wheels came close. "Who cares anyway."

Kay could feel her anger rising. She had had the dog longer than she had had Shayla. She couldn't stand to think that she had brought such terror and pain into its life when she brought this little girl into her home.

"Shayla, you get off the bike and come in the house now," she commanded.

Shayla continued to ride around the yard, ignoring Kay and singing softly to herself.

"Shayla, I'm not kidding. Get off the bike now." Kay's voice carried her anger across the yard.

"No. And you can't make me," Shayla called without bothering to look at Kay.

"Oh, yes I can, young lady," Kay said firmly.

"No, you can't. I won't come in the house, and I won't stop riding my bike. It's my bike, and I can ride it if I want," Shayla shouted.

"You get off that bike right now, Shayla, or else ..." Kay hesitated.

"Or else what?" Shayla called out. That was a question Kay wasn't sure she could answer. At the same time, she didn't feel she could simply turn her back and walk away from her daughter's defiance.

Avoiding and Transforming Power Struggles

Power struggles can ruin your relationship with your child and divide your family into opposing camps. The following tips can help you understand how power struggles develop, so you can stop them before they grow beyond control.

Realize that it is you, not the child, who must take the first step out of the power-struggle dynamic. Your child does not understand that the dynamic between the two of you must change, nor does he understand that there are better, more effective ways to resolve conflict. All he knows is that you want him to do something differently, and he is going to resist.

Accept that it will take time and patience to teach him new conflict resolution skills. Changing this pattern will take more time than you thought. You will be up against your own feelings of anger, and you will be attempting to change reactions that are part of your child's survival skills. This can take months, or even years.

Realize that your child engages in power struggles because he has never experienced a sense of healthy power. He may have felt, and may have been, powerless all of his life. He may fight you over having a bath every night, because that is the only tangible way he can feel in control of his life. It may be that these power struggles are his way of "drawing a line in the sand" and trying to tell you who he is.

Realize that power struggles may be your child's only way of knowing that he is important and that his actions count. Your son may not have enough experience having a positive effect on people to know that he counts in your life. Your child may have only received attention in his past by being loud and angry. If he went to bed when he was told, no one noticed him. If he threw a tantrum, he at least got noticed.

Use conflict as a way of getting to know your child. Power struggles tell you what is important to the child. It may be that the issues you are in conflict over are about the child's need to have some appropriate power, or it may be that it is about his need to feel safe. He may not have the skills to handle the situation another way; perhaps defiance is how he gets rid of intense feelings. Look at what is going on when the power struggle begins; when struggles tend to occur (in the morning or at night); who the struggles are with most of the time; and what allows your child to give in, even a little bit. These are all vital pieces of information about who your child is and what he needs from you.

Check the time. Do you have time for a power struggle right now? Can this issue wait to be worked out at a later time when you are not so rushed or tired? If you make a date to get to this issue with the child later, it will give him time to calm down, and you will have time to consider ways of resolving the situation. You can say, "I know you want me to tell you if you can stay out later with your friends tonight, but I'm in a hurry right now. If we talk about it now, I'll just say 'no.' We can talk about this as soon as I get back from the store."

Realize that the power struggle may be about previous bad experiences. Your child may be refusing to bathe, change clothes, or go to bed, because those were times at which he was abused in the past. He may feel completely vulnerable when alone or undressed. The resistance may be from fear of what you may do to him when he is vulnerable, or it may be from habit.

Take "no" as a negotiating point. When your child says "no," don't take it as such. Turn it into a starting place for negotiations. Instead of saying, "Oh yes you will," say, "Well, if you won't go to bed now, when will you go to bed?" or "What is happening for you now that makes it hard for you to go to bed?" Work from there.

Help your child to "save face" in the power struggle. Your child may be tired of the fight, too, but he doesn't know how to end it. Give him something that will let him get out of the situation with grace. For example, you can say, "If you won't go to bed, will you sleep on the couch?" Or, "You could sleep on the floor, if I get you the sleeping bag, and then you could pretend you are camping out." Or, "If you won't brush your teeth, will you brush your hair and maybe do your teeth when you get home from school?"

Learn to sidestep. When you tell your child to go to bed, and he says "No," you can sidestep by ignoring the no and trying some different responses. For example, if your child refuses to go to bed when you tell him to, you can say, "Do you want me to run your bath first or did you want to skip a bath tonight and read longer in bed?" Or, "Did you say you have clean pajamas or should I check the laundry?" Or, "What happened at school today? Do you want to tell me about it while I straighten your bed?" Or, playfully, "Do you want me to chase you to bed now? Or chase you from the foot of the stairs?"

These are simplistic examples, and as most of you know, your child will often respond to something like this by refusing to move or by swearing at you. However, these examples can give you ideas of how you can sidestep issues right at the beginning, before things get too tense.

Try touching him while you talk. Do not use this suggestion if your child has a history of assault or seems unusually tense. For children who do not respond violently to touch, try putting your hand on his shoulder while you talk. This should be done in an affectionate, not an authoritative manner. He may need to know he is still connected to you, and to let go of some of his stubbornness.

Keep your voice neutral. You need to stay firm, but you can do so without sounding angry or hostile. Don't yell. Don't use sarcasm. Do stay polite.

Avoid trigger issues when possible. If you know your child will not go to bed without a fight, don't tell him to go to bed. Instead, take him by the hand and lead him to bed while talking about other topics. If he is going out for the evening, and you want him in at a time you know he won't agree to, try negotiating a compromise time, a few hours before he is going to go out, rather than telling him what time to be home as he's walking out the door.

Let your child win sometimes. Pick your battles. If this is a child who is going to engage in a power struggle no matter what you do, then pick some battles you can afford to lose, so he gets to experience winning easily on occasion. For example, if he won't go to bed, let him stay up on a Friday night and watch some movies with you.

Give your child some power. Find ways he can be in charge of situations he generally fights over. For example, if he usually refuses to fasten his seat belt, ask him to be in charge of making sure everyone, including himself, is buckled up. If he resists sitting down at the table to eat dinner, try asking him if he wants to be in charge of setting the table or pouring the juice, or if he wants to be the one who says grace before eating.

Let him have the last word. When you have reached some degree of compromise and are able to get past the power struggle, you may find that your child still needs to have the last word. This can feel like the struggle is starting all over again, but it may also be that the child is simply trying to put his own closure on the situation. It could also be his way of keeping some of the power, without getting back into full conflict with you. Either way, if his last word is not rude or aggressive, then leave it alone.

Use basic negotiation skills. Choose a time when you are not fighting, and go though some of the issues that are hot topics. If bathing every night is a trigger for power struggles, negotiate about how much cleanliness your child is willing to have and how much dirt you are willing to let him keep. If your child is smoking, negotiate where he is allowed to smoke, such as outside of the house or at his friend's house, rather than in your house or car. If you cannot get your child to do a reasonable amount of chores, such as making her own bed or cleaning up the table after dinner, work out what she would be willing to do, such as weeding a small patch of garden or watering the plants in the house.

Ask your child to make a snack with you while you talk this over. Some children do not know when they are hungry. The result is a crabby child who is moody due to hunger and low blood sugar. As soon as he says "No," you can say, "I wonder if you're hungry. Do you want to pour some juice while I get us some grapes from the fridge?"

This distracts and cools the anger that is building and gives you both time to take a step back and try another approach to the same issue.

Get away from an audience. If there are other people, or siblings, around, try to move to another room. You will both find it easier to compromise if you do not have an audience.

Sit down. If you have not been able to sidestep or redirect, then sit down and behave as if you are having a formal negotiating discussion. When you stand and are taller than the child, your child can perceive a threat, or a level of authoritarian behavior, that you are not trying to convey.

Avoid power struggles when you are tired. You may be tired most of the time, but do whatever you can to resolve problems while you have some energy and brain power left. Ten o'clock at night is not the time to be discussing whether your teen can get her navel pierced.

Listen to your child's point of view. His point of view may be irrelevant or downright silly, but listen to it fully one time, and then give your response. Don't let him go over and over the same thing, but don't try to stop him from talking until you know he has said it all. When he has finished, thank him for explaining his perspective, then ask him to listen to yours. He may not be willing to do so for the first few months, but repeated episodes of your role-modeling good listening skills will eventually pay off.

Ask what the experience means to your child, rather than why he won't do it. Instead of saying "Why won't you take a bath?" ask, "What happens when you take a bath?" Or instead of saying, "No, you can't stay up all night," you can say, "What is it about going to bed that is difficult for you?" You may have to do this over and over again, before you get the real answer. The child may never have stopped to consider all of the fears and habits that underlie some his resistance to reasonable requests.

Don't moralize, don't use put-downs, and don't preach. These are all adult versions of power struggle tactics that do not lead to compromise, nor positive role-modeling for your child.

Listen to how you are talking to your child. Exhaustion, frustration, and parental feelings of helplessness can put you at risk of slipping into a power struggle with your child, even when you begin a conversation with the intent of staying focused and sidestepping. Keep listening to yourself so you can monitor your tone and words so you can stay in control of yourself and the situation.

Ask your child for his ideas on how to resolve the problem. You can say, "You have to get clean somehow. If you won't bathe, how else can you get clean?" or "If you stay up all night, you will be tired and cranky tomorrow. What can you do so that you won't be tired tomorrow?"

As soon as your child moves the slightest bit toward compromise, notice it and compliment him on his conflict resolution skill. This gives both of you a chance to feel something positive in the encounter. Your child may not recognize that he has made some movement in the discussion and so needs you to bring it to his attention and reinforce it with praise.

Maintain a calm, firm, and respectful tone of voice. Regardless of how rude or confrontational your child behaves, you should maintain the same calm voice that you begin with. It's best if you keep saying the same words, such "Johnny, it's bedtime," rather than "Johnny, this is the fiftieth time I've told you to go to bed."

Expect noncompliance. You should be more surprised when he does not struggle for power than when he does. Your child has survived using this approach all his life, and it should come as no shock to you that he continues trying to survive in the same manner in your home.

CHAPTER 18

Self-Esteem for You and Your Child

There are many definitions of self-esteem. Some people think it means how you see yourself, such as whether you are a good person or a bad person. Others believe it means how you view your skills and your talents and whether you believe you have something to offer to others. Still others believe self-esteem relates to how important and special you believe you are to the people in your life.

In this book, having good self-esteem means that you believe you are important to other people and that you know you are special in many positive ways. It means that you and your child each believe that you are worthy of good treatment by others and that you are able to treat others well. Self-esteem means liking yourself.

The Importance of Self-Esteem

Children who have been abused, neglected, or who have had to live without their own parents, begin to believe that it is their own fault that all these bad things have happened. They begin to believe that they are not important in the world, that they have nothing to offer to others, and that they are invisible and unimportant to others. This belief is painful. It makes the child want to find a way to stop feeling hurt by becoming important and getting noticed. Children who have not developed skills in achieving self-esteem will use whatever they can to get attention. They generally turn to behaviors that are destructive. For children, low self-esteem is often related to poor social and academic skills. That means that areas in which the child finds failure stretch beyond the home. This increases the likelihood that the child will act out in the community and the school.

Signs of Low Self-Esteem

There are many behaviors that accompany low self-esteem. Not all children will exhibit all of the behaviors and not all children will show them in the same way. Some children will display low self-esteem by withdrawing, others by acting out in the home and community. Some behaviors are common in many children with low self-esteem:

- Drug and alcohol abuse
- Suicidal thoughts or attempts
- Slashing their arms or hands
- Withdrawal from friends or family
- Trying to be "invisible"
- Academic underachievement
- Depression
- Sexual activity
- Over-dependence on friendships or a romantic partner
- Teen pregnancy
- Noncompliant behavior
- Refusal to join teams or play with others
- Slow attachment with parents

Signs of High Self-Esteem

Knowing which behavior and attitudes signal healthy self-esteem can help you guide your child toward a higher sense of self-worth. Set attainable goals with your child that will help him experience success and a growing belief in his own abilities. The list below will help you recognize improvements in self-esteem:

- Ability to make decisions
- Sense of responsibility for own actions
- Age- or stage-appropriate social skills
- Appropriate academic achievement
- Appearing happy and responsive
- Trying new things
- Participation in events and activities
- Care about appearance (even though it may not suit your taste)
- Thinking independently of peers
- Developing an attached relationship with you
- Demonstrating appropriate physical affection

Signs of Low Self-Esteem in Adults

Many of the characteristics of low self-esteem displayed by children will also be present in adults with low self-esteem:

- Depression
- Irritability
- Feeling helpless or powerless as a parent
- Lacking initiative in relationships with children in your family
- Isolating self from other adoptive parents of older children
- Inability to see own strengths and accomplishments
- Fear of trying new parenting techniques

Signs of High Self-Esteem in Adults

A parents' sense of high self-esteem is often apparent in their approach to parenting:

- Confidence in parenting skills
- Energetic and enthusiastic about parenting
- Willing to learn and try new parenting techniques

- Awareness of successes in other areas of life

- Stable mood

- Confidence in handling difficult parenting situations

- Willingness to ask for help in dealing with a child's difficult behaviors

The Impact of Esteem on the Family

The problems that are created by your child's low self-esteem can wreak havoc on your family. Difficult behaviors are a major indicator of low self-esteem and these can exhaust and even destroy your family life. Dealing with difficult behaviors can make you feel like a failure as a parent and reduce your coping skills. You can end up with depression and feel that nothing you do that is right for your child.

The characteristics of low self-esteem are similar to characteristics of many other challenges, so even a competent professional can end up misdiagnosing your child's problems. A misdiagnosis will lead to an inappropriate intervention or treatment for your child, and continuing experiences of failure for either you or your child as you attempt to establish your new family.

Low self-esteem will make it difficult for you and your child to develop appropriate attachment. After all, neither of you will want to take the emotional risks that accompany attachment if you don't feel good about yourself as a parent and if your child doesn't feel worthy of your love. Your child may never have had a healthy sense of self-esteem. He may never have understood that he had worth to anyone or that he deserved to be loved. Giving him this view of himself can be difficult, as you'll see in Marcus's story below. Creating healthy self-esteem is one of your most important tasks as a parent.

Life Lesson: Hiding the Pain

Marcus was a good boy. That was the first thing the foster parents had said about him. "He's not like most of the kids we get through here," the foster mother said to Marion on the pre-placement visit. "He's real polite, and he helps out a lot. You won't have any trouble with him."

And five years later, as Marcus maneuvered through the first stages of adolescence, he was still not much trouble. Marcus did reasonably well at school. He had a few friends, although no close buddies. He liked a couple of sports, though he didn't excel at them. He had just started a part-time job sweeping the floor and putting stock on the shelves at the neighborhood hardware store.

"You in there, son?" his dad, Hal, called out. He had come to Marcus's room to tell him it was time for supper. The bedroom door swung open as Hal knocked. His jaw dropped when he saw the room. The mattress was on the floor, and the bedding was all around the room. The window curtains were hanging by one hook, and Marcus's books and CDs were spread from one end of the room to the other.

"What's going on here?" Hal asked. "What have you done?" He took a careful step into the room and saw that Marcus had a kitchen knife in his hand. "Marcus?"

Marcus glared at his father. "I got fired today, Dad. I got fired from a stupid job that an ape could do with its eyes closed."

"Put the knife down, Marcus," Hal said quietly. "Put the knife down, and we can talk about this."

Marcus threw the knife on the bed. "You don't have to be afraid, Dad. If I use the knife, it won't be on anybody except myself."

Hal walked over to the shambles of the bed and sat on the box spring. "What happened at the store?" Hal did not know what to say and he hoped the question was not too naive, or the wrong thing to say. He had never seen his son get really angry before, and he had no idea that Marcus was capable of this kind of behavior.

"I told you, I lost my job. I was too slow." Marcus sank to the floor by his father's feet. "I can't do anything right, Dad. I try so hard, but nothing ever works out properly."

"What do you mean? You do lots of things right. You do well at school, you have friends, you play sports." Hal carefully reached out and touched his son's hair. "And you and I don't fight nearly as much as my friends do with their teens."

"Do you ever read my report card, Dad? It always says, 'Marcus doesn't work up to his potential.' That's the way everything is. I have a couple of friends, but they only hang out with me when no one else is around. And I'm in the loser sports. I never get first pick, and I never get to play in games. I just sit on the bench."

Hal felt his throat tighten. How had he missed these feelings in Marcus? He thought they were close, that he knew his son. He searched for words. "Why do you think you were so slow at the store, son?" He almost bit his tongue as soon as the words were out. What a dumb thing to say, he thought.

"I was slow because I was trying to do it all right. I didn't want to make a mistake." Marcus looked up at his dad. "That's how I do everything, Dad. Slow and careful, so I don't make a mistake. I do what you tell me, so you'll love me. I behave at school, so I won't get in trouble. I check my work ten times, so I don't make too many mistakes. I pick the sports I think I can do, so no one will call me down."

Hal looked into his son's troubled face. He loved this boy more than anything in the world. How had he missed so much pain? And what could he do to make it right?

Creating High Self-Esteem

Building your child's self-esteem creates a foundation that will keep his adult life stable in difficult times. The tips below will help you accomplish this difficult, but essential task.

Spend time alone with your child. When your child knows that you value the time you and he spend together, he will begin to get a sense that he is special and has something to offer to others.

Help your child develop competence. You can do this by giving your child simple tasks in which he can succeed. When assigning chores or tasks around the house, make sure they are ones that the child can do well. And, when he completes them, be sure to comment on the job. For example, if your child cleans the table after dinner, you can say, "You got to that chore really quickly tonight," or "You cleaned up every plate on the table. Good for you."

Help your child understand that people develop at different rates and have different talents and interests, and that qualities that make him different from his peers are what make him special to you. Your child needs to have some understanding of the typical differences between people. He also needs some understanding of how his background may have made him different from his peers in some ways. You cannot assume that he understands this. You will have to help him relearn this at different life stages.

Help your child understand that it is all right to be different. We live in a society that punishes nonconformity and rejects difference. Your child will need to have your help and support to learn that the ways in which he is different do not make him a bad person.

Help your child notice the ways in which he is the same as other children. Your child may only focus on things that are different about him, so he will need your help in recognizing all the ways that he is the same as his peers, as well as all the ways that he is the same as the rest of your family.

Help your child learn to cope with defeats and failures. Everyone is going to fail or lose sometimes, so help your child learn skills so he can do so with grace. You can teach him to try again, to look at other choices, to consider which part of the task he did well, as well as which part he could not complete. Point out that in sports, everyone has a role to play and everyone contributes to the game.

Help your child develop problem-solving skills. If your child is having difficulties with peers, with homework, or with managing his frustration, help him to learn how to solve at least some of the problem on his own. Ask him what he thinks he could do differently to change the situation. Give him some ideas and let him choose one he might try. Ask him how he thinks he might be able to handle the same situation differently the next time. You can even role-play the challenging situation with him, letting him take turns playing himself and playing the other person.

Provide a way for your child to help others. Helping others is a way your child can develop skills and increase his competence. He may be able to volunteer at the local animal shelter one morning a week, or give a weekly grooming to an elderly neighbor's dog. The school or local community center may have volunteer activities that are within the abilities and interests of your child. If not, phone a few local organizations or friends and see if they might know of volunteer activities available to your child.

Be specific in your praise. Telling your child that he has been really good today may reinforce some of his positive behaviors, but it won't help him to understand *how* he has been good, and it won't give him a concrete example of what he can like about himself. Instead of making a vague statement, say, "Your teacher said you really listened in class today," or "I noticed that you didn't hit your sister once today."

Listen to what your child says about his day. Set aside some time each day to chat with your child about how his day went. You can do this after school or in the evening. Try to find a time when there are likely to be few distractions and you can really focus on what he is saying. This will help him to understand that how he experiences his day is important to you. It will also help you to understand where he is succeeding and where he is failing, and will give you clues about the things he fears or his particular areas of vulnerability. You can use that information to help him develop skills for coping with failure or to intervene and help him with areas where he can improve.

Get your child involved in activities. You don't want to overstimulate or exhaust your child, but you can put him in some activities in which he can see his skills improve. For example, swimming lessons provide badges for each level passed. Scouts does the same. Help him practice to improve his skills. If he loves soccer, but is not very good at it, practice with him after school or put him in extra soccer lessons.

Keep your promises. If you promise to fix your child's bike on Saturday, then make sure you do it. If you promise her that she can have a sleepover on Friday night, then make sure it happens. When your child sees that you keep your promises to her, then she will begin to understand how important she is to you.

Let her know how she is expected to behave in social situations, but keep the behavior age- and stage-appropriate. If your child is going to go to a friend's birthday party, teach her the standard behavioral expectations for this type of situation. If you are all going to a family wedding, teach her how to behave there as well. Remember, your older child will not likely have had many opportunities to participate in events or situations in which there are standard expectations of manners. When she succeeds in these situations, she will have yet another reason to feel good about herself. However, keep the expectations and manners at an age- and stage-appropriate level. She is not a little adult, she is a child who may lack social skills, so teach her slowly, and don't expect more than she can reasonably learn.

Increase your child's opportunities for self-reliance. As your child becomes able to undertake activities and complete tasks, reduce the supervision you provide, and let him know that he is able to succeed in some things without your help.

Hug your child and tell him you love him at least once a day. This is likely something you do already. But modern life is very busy, and even our best intentions can go astray. So, make sure you find at least one time in every day to give your child a hug and to say "I love you" in a way that is not rushed and is not offered just because she is going out the door or to bed.

Adults need to pay attention to their self-esteem, too. The daily challenges of living with a difficult child can wear down even the most skilled parents, and make them lose their positive perspective, as Elise discovers in the story below.

Life Lesson: Overwhelmed by the Challenge

It had been a difficult summer. The first few months after nine-year-old Olivier joined the family, things had gone fairly well. He had gone to the neighborhood school, with the other three children in the family, and had attended after-school language programs two days a week. Elise had enrolled him in swimming lessons where he earned his first-level swimming badge, which he proudly displayed on the bulletin board in his room. Both Paul and Elise had felt pretty good about this adoption in those first few months and assumed that since it started off so well, it would continue to do so.

When summer came, they found out just how wrong they were.

Olivier had lived in a highly structured setting his entire life. The orphanage had been run on an unvarying routine, so he had done well with the structure of a regular school year. He knew when to get up; he knew where he was going each day. He was bright and had quickly learned what was expected of him, from teachers and these new parents. Elise had noticed that weekends had been a bit rough, but at the time, she thought it was the typical adjustment behaviors she had heard about. Since nothing really bad had happened, she assumed everything would continue to improve. However, after school had let out for the summer, after just three weeks of less structured time for Olivier, Elise was beside herself with worry and stress.

"I can't stand it, Paul," she told her husband. "He's suddenly destroying his toys, he's hitting the other kids, he's back talking to me every time I tell him he can't do something. I feel like everything is out of my control, and I can't fix it."

Paul knew that Elise was running on empty lately. She had had to put up with the brunt of Olivier's behaviors because she was the parent who was home with him all day. Olivier actually seemed to have a lasting fear of men, so he behaved pretty well once Paul got home from work.

"I know this is hard for you. If I could take any time off, I would, but you know I can't right now. This merger is going to be costly, and if I ask for time off, or try to cut back on my hours so soon after I finished my parental leave, I could lose my job," Paul said as he reached out to take his wife's hand in his. "Is there some other way I can help?"

Elise looked at her husband and sighed. "I know you would do more if you could. I don't think having you home more would fix things, though. I'm just no good at this. I thought that since we adopted the other kids when they were older, that I could manage a nine-year-old."

"The other kids were all under three when we got them, and they had all been in foster homes. This little guy is way older, and doesn't even understand what a family is for. He'll catch on, though. We just have to give him time," Paul said.

Elise sighed again. "How can he catch on when I can't even figure out how to help him?" She pulled her hand away from Paul and looked out the kitchen window, where she could see Olivier swinging listlessly on the tire swing. "I can't bond with him. I can't make him obey me. The other kids are starting to talk back, too, and I can't do anything about that either."

"Well, the other kids are starting to talk back because they've all hit their teens. And I can do something about how they treat you." Paul's support should have felt good, but instead it only made Elise feel less competent.

"You know, sometimes I wonder if my sister was right when we had that spat and she said that the only reason I wanted to adopt again was so I would have an excuse to stay home." Elise could feel the tears at the corner of her eyes. "I mean, the other kids were all doing well and could look after themselves after school. I always said I would go back to work when they hit that stage. Maybe I just couldn't face it, that I couldn't succeed outside of the home."

Paul pushed himself away from the table. "I don't know why you listen to that sister of yours. You two have been squabbling all your lives, and she never has a good thing to say about you. She would jump at any chance to make you feel bad."

"I know, but that doesn't mean she's wrong. I was afraid to go back to work, and I am not doing a good job with Olivier. Now it seems like I can't do a good job with the others either. I don't do anything right anymore. I'm beginning to hate myself."

Retaining Your Self-Esteem

Your self-esteem is essential for maintaining your family's self-esteem. When pressures awaken doubts in your abilities as a parent, or your worth as a person, review and use the suggestions below.

When you are feeling like a failure as a parent to your older child, remind yourself of all the things in your life that you do well. As the parent of an older child, you may find that there are many occasions when you feel that you aren't a good enough parent for your child, or that you lack the patience, tolerance, and stamina to be the kind of parent you thought you would be. That's normal, and at those times, it's best to consider all the other areas in your life where you do well. For example, you may be a wonderful son to your parents, or you may be a good soccer coach, or you may be very skilled at your job outside of the home.

Watch for signs of depression. Depression kills self-esteem. It's not uncommon for parents of older children to go through a stage of depression when the challenges are overwhelming and exhausting. If you find that you are unable to see anything good about who you are, or what you do, go to your doctor and have a checkup for depression.

Do not compare yourself to parents who have typical children. If you have children who have the challenges presented in this book, you don't have the same life as families with typical children. You have more demands on your time, patience, intelligence, compassion, and skills than other moms and dads.

There will be the mom who has one little girl that she adopted at birth, or gave birth to herself, who arrives with her child at school each morning looking fresh and well groomed, carrying twenty-six cupcakes for the whole class, or chatting about how late she was up last night, making lists for one of the parenting groups she chairs. You, on the other hand, may have arrived at school after dealing with a raging child who wouldn't get dressed, who threw her cereal against the wall, who wouldn't fasten her seat belt, and who threatened to call the child-protection authorities if you made her put on her jacket. Just appreciate that you made it to the school at all. Be glad there is someone to make the cupcakes and the lists, since you don't have the spare time to do it. Just appreciate it, and get on with your day.

Enhance your parenting skills. You may need to learn more skills in order to feel good about being a parent to your child. Taking communication or anger-management courses or attending adoption conferences will help you to develop more effective parenting skills, and increase your positive feelings about how you parent your older child.

Accept praise from others. People may tell you that you are a good parent to your child, but you hesitate to accept this. Don't argue or shrug it off. Instead, say "Thank you," and let yourself indulge a little bit in the good feelings that go with such a compliment.

Keep a bottom-line chart. Make a list of all the challenges your child is facing and date it. Break the list down into specific behaviors. For example, if your child has reactive attachment disorder, write down all the ways your child shows this, such as "lies more than twice a day," "will not accept hugs," "says 'I hate you' every night," "hurts the pets," or "never bathes without a rage." As each of these improves, note the date and check it off. This will give you a concrete way of seeing the changes and realizing that you are having a positive impact on your child.

Have fun in your life. Laughing and taking pleasure in life keeps self-esteem high. No matter how much stress you are under from your child's challenging behaviors, make sure you have some part of your life that is fun. You may find that going to good movies gives you this lift, or perhaps attending concerts, or being with favorite friends.

Exercise. The overall health benefits of exercise are well known. However, an often forgotten benefit is that exercise is a natural mood enhancer as well as a healthy form of stress reduction.

CHAPTER 19

General Survival Tips

Children who are placed in an adoptive home at an older age will have problems of some kind. The old adage "If it seems too good to be true, it is" applies here. If the child presented to you appears to be "perfect," then you should expect that some major issues will surface, as the child learns to relax and trust in your ability to help her and keep her safe. Despite the inevitable adjustments and challenges, you can still have a wonderful and fulfilling relationship with your child, but she will arrive in your life with a history of trauma and abandonment, and you will have to help her work past this.

Social workers and adoptive parents often think that because the pre-placement visits went well and occurred over a long period of time, there will be few if any adjustment issues. Others believe that when they see that magical instant bonding occur, a problem-free adjustment period will follow. It is not unusual for people to believe that if the child had a relatively smooth pre-placement life, and doesn't have psychological disorders, there is no reason to expect problems when he is older.

Unfortunately, all children and families will have some adjusting to do, and there will be problems that the family did not anticipate. If they don't occur right at the beginning of the placement, problems may occur six months, a year, or two years later, when the child begins to feel safe enough to drop his defenses and begins to experience the long-term effects of his early trauma.

Some parents know ahead of time that their child has serious behavioral problems and think that this knowledge will protect them from the frustration and conflicting feelings that generally accompany older-child placements. But even realistic expectations don't help during those nights when you can't sleep for fear of the child burning down the house, or because she has just been suspended from school and neither you nor your spouse can take time off work to stay home with her.

The techniques noted in this book will help significantly, but there are still some things that you can do to survive the years that it may take for the child and the family to adjust to each other, and to overcome, or learn to live with, the challenges.

Family Survival Techniques

The following tips will help you through your rough first year with your older child, as well as help you weather storms that arise in the future.

Find and use appropriate therapy. The whole family will need professional help, not just the child. You and the other children in the family, and even involved grandparents, may need help learning to adjust to and live with the ongoing challenges. But make certain that the therapist is trained in adoption-specific issues. And don't take his or her word for it. Grill her like you would a plumber or house builder. Get references from other adoptive parents. Also, beware of the therapist who spends most of his time with the child. It's very easy for a vulnerable child to bond with a therapist. After all, the therapist isn't threatening. He or she dedicates the hour to the child, and doesn't present any of his or her own needs. However, if the child is placing all of her trust in the therapist, then she isn't placing it in you.

The role of the therapist is to help you learn to gain the trust of your child, not to gain that trust themselves. And the task of the adoption therapist is to help you learn to manage the behaviors of your child. A large portion of the therapeutic time should be spent teaching you what to do, then providing support and coaching while you learn how to do it.

A therapist should also help your child find solutions to her painful feelings and memories. Repeatedly processing past traumas is not helping the child develop the skills and resources she needs in order to develop attachment and then function in a socially acceptable manner.

If your community doesn't have a therapist who specializes in adoption, then find a therapist who is willing to learn, and suggest that he or she contact an adoption specialist who is willing to supervise the case by telephone or e-mail. There are several qualified therapists who advertise on the Internet and may be willing to provide supervision, for a fee.

Join or create a local adoptive-parents' association. Local adoption agencies will know how to get in touch with adoptive-parent associations. Also, join a few adoption related mailing lists (both print and e-mail). It's important that you don't feel isolated from other families who can help you find the joy in your small victories. There are several national adoption newsletters and magazines that help families understand the larger picture of adoption, and provide information on national and regional conferences. Appropriate support can come only from other families living the same life.

Attend national and regional conferences. Conferences will help you learn about the challenges that are unique to adoption, and to the placement of older children. Families who adopt older children require a thorough, correct understanding of their children's challenges. Conferences can provide a much needed refueling for you, helping you develop a support network, as well as presenting speakers who teach methods of managing behaviors and relationships.

Hire baby-sitters who have professional training. Recruit baby-sitters from a local licensed daycare, or from a university program that teaches child care or early childhood education. These people cost more, but they provide a level of skill and patience that the teen on the block, or the well-meaning grandparent, simply does not have.

Stand united. A child who can't feel loyalty will often try to control his life situation by creating tension and disagreement between his parents. The child can't understand the damage this can do; he can only understand that this is a means of getting what he thinks he needs. It's important that you and your spouse deal with conflicts and disagreements over child-related issues without appearing to side with the child against the other parent. You can argue it out in the therapist's office or when you are out to lunch together. The situations in which the child is trying to divide you are actually teaching moments. If he can observe you two remaining disengaged from his attempts to restructure the power balance in the family, he will learn that you both mean what you say, and are able to stay in charge without resorting to violence or rejection.

Ally with your child to manage the problem. With the help of an adoption-oriented therapist, help your child define and understand the challenges he is dealing with. Once your child has the concept, you can start using language to help him grasp that this is something everyone in the family can work on together. It can almost take on the form of a project. For example, when a child with attachment issues is being noncompliant for the sole purpose of rejecting you, then you can say, "Okay, so you need to reject me right now. Do you have any ideas on what we can do together to get past this?" More than likely, he will say "no" or swear or scream or bite or try to tear the ear off the dog or behave in some other manner that continues the rejection. You can then use a consequence that is appropriate to the behavior, but do so in a calm manner, using language that tells the child what is happening. For example, you can say, "Well, I guess I have to come up with an idea myself, and my idea is that you can have time-out at the table for fifteen minutes. Let's get your crayons and coloring books." When the time-out is over, you can say, "We almost got past the attachment challenge this time. Good for us."

This same process can be used for children who are aggressive or who have fetal alcohol syndrome or attention deficit disorder. Name the challenge, acknowledge that both of you handled it well this time, or acknowledge how you or your child could have managed it better. This is a simplified example, but can be tailored to any behavior and any situation. The important thing is to let your child know that this is a family challenge, not his or her individual problem.

Leave the child at home or in respite for some family vacations or occasions. If vacations or high-stimulus times are triggers for your child, leave him at home with a caregiver while the rest of the family goes to the seashore, attends the wedding, or goes out to dinner. You and the other children have a right to create some positive memories of family times, and the acting-out child has the right to remain in a controlled and safe situation.

Avoid social isolation. Many families who adopt older children find that after the child arrives, their friends gradually drift away. Avoid this by making a concerted effort to educate friends and extended family on the special issues that are now part of your family life. Friends will be more likely to stay involved in your family's life if they understand and become comfortable with the differing concerns. Begin or continue interests that are not adoption related, such as bowling, bird watching, etc. Make sure there is time for activities that keep you and your spouse in contact with others on a social basis.

CHAPTER 20

Putting It All Together

You probably entered into adoption because you wanted a child, or because you wanted more children than you already had. There may be unique and complex psychological, sociological, and biological reasons underlying your decision, but it all boils down to the simple matter of wanting a child. However, when you create a family, for whatever reason and by whatever means, you are also fulfilling a larger role in society. You are helping to raise productive citizens who will, hopefully, be an asset to the community when they reach adulthood.

When you adopt an older child, you are also taking on the moral, spiritual, physical, and intellectual challenge of compensating for all that your child has suffered before. It becomes your responsibility to see that your older child has all of the support and services she needs to heal from the trauma of her past and to find her place in society.

One of the main tasks of the family unit is to give its children a sense of *belonging* in the world. Your family will provide your child with the understanding that he has a right to exist and is entitled to grow and to experiment with life. Most importantly, you will give your child the belief that he is irreplaceable.

Replacing Aloneness with Belonging

Children who have spent even one day without a permanent family lose their sense of foundation and the sense of entitlement that goes with it. In order to survive, children who have been neglected and are without permanent families innately understand that they must quickly develop the ability to navigate the world alone, because learning how to be *alone* is the skill that will keep them alive.

Every ability that the waiting child develops is an outgrowth of learning to be alone. The waiting child must put all of his energy, abilities, and talents into treading water in a sea of emotional confusion and loneliness. The first and only survival skill he must develop is the ability to sail alone through each of the issues that will challenge his life.

Attachment, for children who have permanent families, is a pathway to loving others and developing relationships. The child without parents can only face this challenge by accepting that he is truly alone in the world. The losses that will confront him at every turn in his life force him to develop skills to survive alone with his grief. Behaviors that are aggressive or sexually intrusive reinforce the child's belief that only he can find a way to meet his needs. Conditions such as attention deficit disorder or fetal alcohol syndrome create behaviors that force him to live emotionally alone. As he tries to fit into each foster family, and then a new adoptive family, he will be challenged by how different his identity is from that of the others in the group, and he will learn to be alone within his new family. The child with cross-cultural or transracial issues will have to develop skills to be alone with his facial structure, the color of his skin, or the memory of his original culture. The child who faces temporary adoption disruption will be reinforced in his knowledge that he exists alone in the world. And the child who is dealing with adoptive parents experiencing an "oops response" will have his aloneness reinforced on a daily basis.

The challenge for the adopting parents is to help the child move from a sense of existing alone in the universe, to learning the skills of belonging. The challenge of attachment then becomes the task of helping the child let go of aloneness, even before the issues are resolved or the love can be expressed. The loss and grief may not ever be resolved for the child, but he can move on to belonging by learning that emotional pain doesn't kill, that it can be lived with, and that the past doesn't have to control the present. The child who exhibits aggressive or sexually intrusive behaviors has the opportunity, through professional therapy and parental support, to learn that trauma can be resolved, that limits can be accepted, and that no one has the right to harm others. The child with ADD or FAS can learn to recognize and develop his strengths. The process of family identity formation helps the child to learn that he can contribute to the development of a family, that he has a role in creating who this new adoptive unit is becoming. The child with cross-cultural or transracial issues can learn that he is still connected to his origins in many ways, that others share his background and culture, and that the differences he brings to the family are ultimately transformed into the strengths that hold the family together. Families who face temporary disruptions can help the child learn that he alone is not the problem, that together they all have new skills and abilities to learn. The child who has watched his parents resolve and grow from the "oops" phase will be reinforced in his sense of importance to the family.

The Greatest Challenge of Them All

The real challenge of older-child adoption is not one of overcoming differing problems, genetics, or pasts; rather, it is one of moving the child away from feeling alone and toward a sense of belonging. Parents must provide the child a foundation that will allow him to learn that he has an important place in the adoptive family, and that he is entitled to the time, the commitment, and the support he needs to create his unique place in the universe.

There is something present in your eyes when you look at your child. It isn't present when you look at anyone else. It's not a look that you create on purpose, and it doesn't go away when you are angry with your child. He doesn't see that expression in the eyes of anyone else in the world. Every child needs to see that look in someone. But your child may never have seen it until he came to live with you. Giving him the opportunity to see that look in your eyes when he stands before you is the only real gift you have to offer, and it is the best gift that he will ever receive.

References

Kubler-Ross, Elisabeth. 1969. *On Death and Dying*. New York: Macmillan Publishing Company.

Perry, Bruce D. 1999. Post-traumatic Stress Disorders in Children and Adolescents. *Current Opinions in Pediatrics* 11.

McBurnett, Keith. 2000. Prefrontal Gray Matter Volume and Reduced Automatic Activity in Antisocial Personality Disorder. *Archives of General Psychiatry* 57:38–43.

Brenda McCreight, Ph.D., is a family and child therapist and an adoption expert with more than twenty year's experience. She specializes in pre- and postadoption issues including counseling for adoptive and foster families in crisis and for families and children dealing with challenges such as fetal alcohol syndrome, ADHD, conduct disorder, attachment disorder, developmental delays, and cognitive impairment. McCreight is also an adult educator for both professional and lay audiences on issues related to child development, child trauma, adoptive and foster family relationships, and child behavior disorders. She lives in Nanaimo, British Columbia with her partner; they have nine children, seven of whom were adopted as older children.

Some Other
New Harbinger Titles

The 50 Best Ways to Simplify Your Life, Item FWSL $11.95

When Anger Hurts Your Relationship, Item WARY $13.95

The Couple's Survival Workbook, Item CPSU $18.95

Loving Your Teenage Daughter, Item LYTD $14.95

The Hidden Feeling of Motherhood, Item HFM $14.95

Parenting Well When Your Depressed, Item PWWY $17.95

Thinking Pregnant, Item TKPG $13.95

Pregnancy Stories, Item PS $14.95

The Co-Parenting Survival Guide, Item CPSG $14.95

Family Guide to Emotional Wellness, Item FGEW $24.95

How to Survive and Thrive in an Empty Nest, Item NEST $13.95

Children of the Self-Absorbed, Item CSAB $14.95

The Adoption Reunion Survival Guide, Item ARSG $13.95

Undefended Love, Item UNLO $13.95

Why Can't I Be the Parent I Want to Be?, Item PRNT $12.95

Kid Cooperation, Item COOP $14.95

Breathing Room: Creating Space to Be a Couple, Item BR $14.95

Why Children Misbehave and What to do About it, Item BEHV $14.95

Couple Skills, Item SKIL $15.95

The Power of Two, Item PWR $15.95

The Queer Parent's Primer, Item QPPM $14.95

Illuminating the Heart, Item LUM $13.95

Dr. Carl Robinson's Basic Baby Care, Item DRR $10.95

The Ten Things Every Parent Needs to Know, Item KNOW $12.95

Call **toll free, 1-800-748-6273,** or log on to our online bookstore at **www.newharbinger.com** to order. Have your Visa or Mastercard number ready. Or send a check for the titles you want to New Harbinger Publications, Inc., 5674 Shattuck Ave., Oakland, CA 94609. Include $4.50 for the first book and 75¢ for each additional book, to cover shipping and handling. (California residents please include appropriate sales tax.) Allow two to five weeks for delivery.

Prices subject to change without notice.